Bringing Poetry Alive

Education at SAGE

SAGE is a leading international publisher of journals, books, and electronic media for academic, educational, and professional markets.

Our education publishing includes:

- accessible and comprehensive texts for aspiring education professionals and practitioners looking to further their careers through continuing professional development

- inspirational advice and guidance for the classroom

- authoritative state of the art reference from the leading authors in the field

Find out more at: **www.sagepub.co.uk/education**

Bringing Poetry Alive
A Guide To Classroom Practice

Edited by
Michael Lockwood

Los Angeles | London | New Delhi
Singapore | Washington DC

First published 2011

SAGE Publications Ltd
1 Oliver's Yard
55 City Road
London EC1Y 1SP

SAGE Publications Inc.
2455 Teller Road
Thousand Oaks, California 91320

SAGE Publications India Pvt Ltd
B 1/I 1 Mohan Cooperative Industrial Area
Mathura Road
New Delhi 110 044

SAGE Publications Asia-Pacific Pte Ltd
33 Pekin Street #02-01
Far East Square
Singapore 048763

Library of Congress Control Number: 2010940991

British Library Cataloguing in Publication data

A catalogue record for this book is available from the British Library

ISBN 978-0-85702-073-4
ISBN 978-0-85702-074-1 (pbk)

Typeset by C&M Digitals (P) Ltd, Chennai, India
Printed in Great Britain by CPI Antony Rowe, Chippenham, Wiltshire
Printed on paper from sustainable resources

MIX
Paper from
responsible sources
FSC
www.fsc.org   FSC® C013604

For all the colleagues and students I have shared poetry with at
the University of Reading over the past 21 years

ML

Contents

Acknowledgements

Thanks are due to:

Lorna Anderton and her Reception class for the case study contained in Chapter 2.
Those English teachers working in the borough of Wokingham who helped in the preparation of Chapter 7.
Cheam School, The Emmbrook School, and The Bulmershe School for permission to reproduce children's work.
The parents of Jack Brown and of Isobel Owen for permission to reproduce their children's work.

I'm also grateful to the following who have kindly given permission to reproduce copyrighted material here.
Billy Collins, excerpt from 'Introduction to Poetry' from *The Apple That Astonished Paris*. Copyright © 1988, 1996 by Billy Collins. Used by permission of the University of Arkansas Press, www.uapress.com
'Louder!' by Roger Stevens, from *Performance Poems*, ed. Brian Moses (Southgate, 1996), included by permission of the author.
'Neil Armstrong' and 'Count Dracula' © John Foster 2000, 2007, from *The Poetry Chest* (Oxford University Press), included by permission of the author.
'My Rabbit' and 'Cobweb Morning' © 2005 June Crebbin, from *The Crocodile is Coming* by June Crebbin. Reproduced by permission of Walker Books Ltd, London, SE1 5HJ.
'Shallow Poem' © Gerda Mayer: from *The Knockabout Show* (Chatto & Windus, 1978), first published in the magazine *Ambit* (1971). Reprinted by permission of the author.
The Literary Trustees of Walter de la Mare and The Society of Authors as their representative for the excerpt from 'Dream Song' by Walter de la Mare.

About the Editor and Contributors

Editor

Michael Lockwood taught in schools in Oxford before becoming Senior Lecturer in English and Education at the University of Reading, where he is now co-director of the BA(Ed) programme. His publications include *A Study of the Poems of D.H. Lawrence: Thinking in Poetry* (1987), *Opportunities for English in the Primary School* (1996) and *Promoting Reading for Pleasure in the Primary School* (SAGE, 2008), which won him the United Kingdom Literacy Association's Author Award for 2009. He has also published classroom poetry resources and anthologies and has written his own poems for children.

Contributors

James Carter is a children's poet and an educational writer. He has a BA(Ed) and MA in Children's Literature from the University of Reading. He travels all over the UK and abroad to visit schools, libraries and book festivals for performances, workshops, writing residencies and INSET sessions. His poetry collections include *Cars, Stars, Electric Guitars* (Walker Books), *Time-Travelling Underpants, and Greetings, Earthlings!* (Macmillan) and *Hey, Little Bug!* (Frances Lincoln). Over the last 10 years, James has written four widely used and critically acclaimed creative writing books for teachers of 7–14-year-olds. His website is www.jamescarterpoet.co.uk

Prue Goodwin is a freelance lecturer in literacy and children's books and formerly Lecturer in Primary English at the University of Reading. Her work, which takes her all over the UK and beyond, involves presenting keynote sessions at conferences, organising courses, acting as a consultant to publishers of children's books and researching literacy learning in schools. Before becoming a lecturer, Prue taught poetry of all sorts to all age groups in primary and middle schools for over 20 years. She has edited several books on teaching English, including *The Literate Classroom* (David Fulton, 2005) and *Understanding Children's Books: A Guide for Education Professionals* (SAGE, 2008).

Andy Goodwyn is Professor of Education at The University of Reading. Having taught secondary English in schools, he then ran both PGCE Secondary and Masters programmes in English Education at the University before becoming Head of its Institute of Education. He has presented on English teaching around the world and written many articles and books. Recent publications include *The Expert Teacher of English* (2010), and *The Great Literacy Debate* (2011).

Eileen Hyder has many years of teaching experience across all age ranges, in both state and independent schools. She has organised a number of poetry events within schools, including workshops with visiting poets and poetry presentations. For three years she organised the SATIPS (Support and Training in Prep Schools) poetry competition and has published articles on poetry writing. She is studying for a PhD in researching reading groups for visually-impaired people at the University of Reading, where she was appointed Lecturer in Primary English in 2010.

Andy Kempe is Senior Lecturer in Drama Education at the University of Reading. He has extensive experience of working in drama with pupils of all ages and has been providing INSET to Drama and English teachers throughout the country and abroad for many years. He has written numerous articles and chapters covering a wide spectrum of issues in drama and his books are standard texts in a great many schools. He is the author of *The GCSE Drama Coursebook* and co-author of *Speaking, Listening and Drama, Progression in Secondary Drama* and *Learning to Teach Drama 11–18*.

Catriona Nicholson was, for many years, a teacher in primary and special schools before becoming a Lecturer in English and Children's Literature at the University of Reading. She has been a co-director of the Centre for Research into Childhood: Literature, Culture, Media at Reading and was a tutor on the MA course in Children's Literature. Having retired from undergraduate teaching, she is now a Trustee of Seven Stories: the Centre for the Children's Book in Newcastle. Recent publications include contributions to *Literacy through Creativity* (ed. P. Goodwin, 2004), *Twentieth-Century Literary Criticism* (eds T. Schoenberg and L. Trudeau, Thomson Gale, 2006), *Understanding Children's Books* (ed. P. Goodwin, SAGE, 2008) and *The Literate Classroom*, 3rd edn (ed. P. Goodwin, Routledge, 2010).

Margaret Perkins, a former primary school headteacher, is currently Lecturer in Education and Assistant Director of the University of Reading's Graduate Teacher Programme (Primary). She is currently researching, with Prue Goodwin, the use of reading aloud in primary teaching. Recent publications include: 'Inside the Classroom' in M. Lewis and S. Ellis (eds) *Phonics: Practice, Research and Policy* (PCP, 2006), 'Making Space for Reading' in P. Goodwin (ed.) *The Literate Classroom* (Routledge, 2005), 'Literacy, Creativity and Popular Culture' in P. Goodwin (ed.) *Literacy Through Creativity* (David Fulton, 2004) and *Observing Primary Literacy* (SAGE, 2011).

Michael Rosen first started writing poetry when he was about 15, inspired by reading D.H. Lawrence, Gerard Manley Hopkins, Carl Sandburg and James Joyce's *Portrait of the Artist as a Young Man*. He zig-zagged through education after that, doing Arts A-levels, going to medical school and then doing a degree in English at Oxford University. He also has an MA in Children's Literature from the University of Reading. His first book of poetry for children was *Mind Your Own Business* (Andre Deutsch, 1974) and since then he has been publishing poetry and performing it in schools, libraries, theatres and colleges. He was Children's Laureate from 2007–09. Some of his poetry performances are on his website: www.michaelrosen.co.uk

Morag Styles is Reader in Children's Literature at the University of Cambridge. She has written and lectured widely on children's poetry. She has organised many international conferences on children's literature as well as being responsible for a major exhibition at the British Library in 2009 (with Michael Rosen) on the history of poetry for children. She is the author of *From the Garden to the Street: 300 Years of Poetry for Children* (Cassell, 1998) and co-editor of *Poetry and Childhood* (Trentham, 2010). She was an External Examiner at the University of Reading from 2007–09.

Lionel Warner teaches English to secondary trainee teachers at the University of Reading, and runs the Overseas Trained Teacher Programme. Before that he taught English for 30 years in secondary schools. He has senior examination experience in English Literature at all three secondary key stages, and has published a number of articles for English teachers, including 'Asking the Right Question: Some Aspects of the Assessment of English Literature' in *Changing English* (Routledge, vol. 16, 2009).

Preface

Morag Styles

In Tune with Yourself: Teachers, Pupils, Poets

Like one of the contributors to this volume, in my early career I experienced the groans of children after being told that they were going to do poetry. I soon learned to beguile the class into loving poetry by reading poems that would please them – without any warning – and getting them to read, perform and write their own, as well as collect their favourites in class anthologies. I managed quite happily with classic poetry, early Ted Hughes *(Meet My Folks)*, Charles Causley and the many talented poets writing for children in the first half of the twentieth century. However, things really took off once *Mind Your Own Business* appeared in 1974, the first of Michael Rosen's very successful collections for children. His volume started a new trend; after that, there was never a problem with getting the pupils on side for poetry. One could then extend the range as pupils' ears got tuned to poetry, and soon it was possible to tackle almost any poem I wanted to share with children.

I wrote a couple of books for teachers, long out of print, to encourage others to believe in children as writers and readers of poetry. One was called *In Tune with Yourself* (Dunn et al., 1986) and that strikes me as a good title for this Preface as all the contributors to this volume will appreciate. They know that what good poetry teachers try to do is to help children find their own voices, as well as offering them access to a body of work stretching back as far as the beginnings of print and including the oral tradition. They also know that in the best and worst moments of our lives, poetry is a resource and solace, while at less pressured times, it can amuse us, make us think of things we always knew but had forgotten (Robert Frost) or bed the ear with a kind of literary hard core that can be built on (Seamus Heaney). A profound belief in the good offices of poetry permeates this welcome new volume.

The title says it all. Enthusiasts for *Bringing Poetry Alive*, all with some connection to the University of Reading's Institute of Education, show how to promote poetry joyfully in the classroom and beyond. The perspectives of poets, teachers, teacher educators and a Children's Laureate combine to offer the reader a whole range of practical ideas for making poetry an enjoyable and satisfying experience with the young. All the contributors share a love of poetry combined with expertise in using it creatively with children. What is more, they show respect for, and belief in, the amazing things children can achieve in reading, writing, listening to and performing poetry, if it is tackled with flair and imagination. Teachers new to poetry need not be afraid – this book is very approachable and will help them find their ways into effective poetry teaching. For seasoned practitioners, there are fresh ideas and the companionship of kindred spirits.

Michael Lockwood is the guiding hand behind this harvest of poetry practice. He has been a quiet aficionado of children's poetry for many years and it is fitting that SAGE has given him the opportunity to put this volume together. In his Introduction, Michael sets out something of the history of poetry teaching in England. Some of that story is quite depressing, as poetry has always challenged teachers; it is less well covered (and, research suggests, less well taught – see recent work by Teresa Cremin and colleagues) than most other literary genres in primary and secondary classrooms – right up to 'A' level. Michael Rosen talks of his concern to break out of the cycle where schools teach for tests and cut down time and space for reading 'real books' and engaging in other forms of creative learning. (Indeed, our new government, which talks of freedom for schools, is actually strengthening its grip on the curriculum in areas like the teaching of phonics.) But as both the 'Michaels' writing in this book make clear, there are also grounds for optimism.

Rosen made a huge impact on children's poetry as Laureate and some of his initiatives are documented here. As I write, I am aware of other promising developments. At least 10 new single poet collections for children are either going into print or have recently been published. T.S. Eliot award-winner, Philip Gross' *Off Road to Everywhere* is an excellent example, part of a set of six collections of children's poetry by his publisher, Salt. Janetta Otter-Barry has four new titles on her list for Frances Lincoln – and there is more in the pipeline from Macmillan and A & C Black. A new volume on Caribbean poetry aimed at 11–16-year-olds is under construction at Peepal Tree Press at the moment. On my bookshelf, three recently published collected poems for children by brilliant poets nestle together – Adrian Mitchell (much missed), Allan Ahlberg and the Poet Laureate, Carol Ann Duffy. (The latter won the Centre for Literacy in Primary Education (CLPE) Poetry Award, 2010, with her *New and Collected Poems for Children*.) Sue Dymoke at Leicester University has recently been successful in getting funding for an Economic and Social Research Council seminar series on teaching poetry, while David Whitley at Cambridge University's Faculty of Education is starting a British Academy funded project on how teachers tackle poetry with students from Reception to university. Several competitions for children as poets/children as anthologists, as well as awards for new collections of poetry for young readers, are soon to be publicised. And, unusually, we have two edited volumes on children's poetry being published within the same year – this book and my own, *Poetry and Childhood* (2010, co-edited with Louise Joy and David Whitley).

Decades ahead of his time (in 1956) Ted Hughes wrote a letter to Sylvia Plath anticipating the knowledge we have gained from neuroscience about the uses of the brain:

And Eliot says that the best thing a poet can do is read aloud poetry ... This should be sound. Silent reading only employs the parts of the brain that are used in vision. Not all the brain. This means that a silent reader's literary sense becomes detached from the motor parts and the audio parts of the brain which are used in reading aloud – tongue and ear. This means that only a third of the mental components are present in their writing or in their understanding of reading. (Hughes, quoted in Reid, 2007: 50)

This book requires every contributor to conclude their chapter by giving the reader 'something to think about', 'something to read' and 'something to do'. No parts of the brain falling idle here. Put one in every staffroom!

Morag Styles
Reader in Children's Literature and Education
University of Cambridge
December 2010

References

Cremin, T., Mottram, M., Collins, F., Powell, S. and Safford, K. (2009) *Teachers as Readers: Building Communities of Readers*. London: United Kingdom Literacy Association.

Dunn, J., Styles, M. & Warburton, N. (1986) *In Tune with Yourself*. Cambridge: Cambridge University Press.

Duffy, C.A. (2009) *New and Collected Poems for Children*. London: Faber and Faber.

Gross, P. (2010) *Off Road to Everywhere*. Cambridge: Salt.

Reid, C. (2007) *Letters of Ted Hughes*. London: Faber and Faber.

Rosen, M. (1974) *Mind Your Own Business*. London: Bodley Head.

Styles, M., Joy, L. & Whitley, D. (2010) *Poetry and Childhood*. Stoke-on-Trent: Trentham.

Introduction

Michael Lockwood

A Tale of Two English Teachers

Mr Platt and Mr Boon taught me English in the early years of secondary school, between the ages of 11 and 14. It was the 1960s and I was a pupil at a boys' grammar school in the West Riding of Yorkshire, a region where, unknown to me, a sea-change was taking place in the teaching of English, particularly the teaching and assessment of writing.

As I look back through my English schoolbooks of this time, when I was 11 and 12, Mr Platt's comments on my written work recall his approach: *write an essay, not a story (4/10); careless (6/10); fair effort (6/10); too brief (4/10); a capital letter is not required in the same sentence.* Mr Platt's response to one piece of writing, 'A Seaside Resort in the Rain', still sticks in my mind. I have S.S. (*sentence structure*) written in the margin six times and a mark of 9 minus 3 out of 10 at the end (presumably losing half a mark per S.S.!). No other comment is given. I remember being particularly proud of this descriptive piece and of lines such as 'Rain playing a continuous tune on the pavements with an occasional plop as it entered a puddle', which received an S.S.

When I was 13, Mr Boon entered my school life and a different kind of English teaching arrived with him. Mr Boon was informal, zany even, in teaching style and speech – within the limits of a state grammar school where 'masters' still wore gowns and honours boards still hung in the hall. We were given what then seemed weird and wonderful topics to write about in prose and poetry: 'Conversation between a Bank Clerk and a Gangster', 'You Cannot Escape Death!'; we read war poets and wrote our own war poems; we wrote fictional autobiographies. My writing began to be appreciated, my marks went up and the comments in my English book changed: *good (8/10); well recounted (8/10); excellent, splendid vocabulary (9/10); you have improved so much. The first half of this is splendid (9/10).* The written comments hardly do justice to Mr Boon's impact on me and my peers; most of the feedback that counted was oral. The way my marks continued to improve in mockery of the school's very basic assessment system gives a better impression of his approach: 10/10, 12/10, 13/10, 25/20.

With the change from Mr Platt to Mr Boon, my English teaching changed from a policing of the subject, with an expectation of conformity and a meticulous accounting of any infringements, to encouragement of individuality and a valuing of creativity and imagination. So the creative writing movement of the 1960s came into my education, though looking back it was in a fairly diluted form. I've searched my English books in vain for free verse poems, but all are doggedly (not to say doggerelly) rhyming. I don't recall any lessons where fires were started in wastepaper baskets or staged arguments broke out between teachers to provide 'stimulus' for our writing, and I've failed to find any examples of my writing in Chief Education Officer Alec Clegg's landmark collection of West Riding pupils' work, *The Excitement of Writing* (1964). However, excitement *did* come into English with Mr Boon – poetry teaching *was* brought to life, and the impact of this has stayed with me ever since: hence this book.

I'd like to begin by reviewing where this development in my own education came from and then, in the remainder of this Introduction, to trace how poetry teaching has developed since this time.

Developments in Poetry Teaching

1940s, 1950s and 1960s

Richard Andrews, in his aptly titled *The Problem with Poetry* (1991), has charted the development of poetry teaching in English schools since the Second World War. He has shown how the pioneering work of Marjorie Hourd in *The Education of the Poetic Spirit* (1949) and James Britton in his writings on the 'poetic function' of language led to the creative writing or 'progressive' movement in schools which brought Mr Boon into my classroom and was exemplified by publications such as those of Alec Clegg and Michael Baldwin's *Poetry without Tears* (1959) (Andrews, 1991: 26–8). Baldwin's comment: 'The classroom is not a lecture room; still less is it a courtroom. At most it is a workshop, with the teacher the master craftsman' (1959: 99) can stand as representative for the teaching approach of this movement. Poets such as C. Day Lewis (1944) and James Reeves (1958) also contributed to these developments in books aimed at children and teachers respectively, Lewis stressing pleasure and Reeves 'personal enthusiasm', 'liveliness and variety', demonstrated in collaborative work and 'active enjoyment', as key factors in teaching poetry (Reeves, 1958: 10–11). Over half a century on, this still sounds relevant to today's debates about poetry teaching and learning, as witnessed by many of the contributors to this volume.

Andrews (1991: 68–73) also mentions the significant contributions of later poets such as Ted Hughes and the American Kenneth Koch to poetry teaching in the 1960s and early 1970s in publishing practical poetry teaching manuals which were also anthologies of poetry for the classroom and writing by children. Hughes' approach has connections with the creative writing movement. His

Poetry in the Making (1967), based on earlier BBC schools radio broadcasts he made in 1961–62, famously described the premise he worked from in his talks as an assumption that 'the latent talent for self-expression in any child is immeasurable', though he acknowledged the practical difficulties of such an assumption in the classroom. For Hughes, the important thing for teachers to stress to children was not 'How to write' but 'How to try to say what you really mean' (Hughes, 1967: 12). His recommended method for teachers to use with children was very much Hughes' own as a poet: 'headlong, concentrated improvisation on a set theme' within a short timescale, 'showing to a pupil's imagination many opportunities and few restraints.' (pp. 12, 23). This can produce 'the kind of writing children can do without becoming false to themselves', which is the danger when children are asked to use established literary models for their own writing (p. 12).

Koch's approach in *Wishes, Lies and Dreams* (first published 1970) and *Rose, Where Did You Get That Red?* (1973), based on his work as a visiting poet in New York schools, is different. Whereas Hughes stresses spontaneity and a lack of constraints other than time and length, Koch offers young poets simple, non-rhyming structures to work within, such as 'list poems' using repeated phrases in each line, for example 'I wish I was ...' , 'I dreamed ...', or 'I used to be ... but now ...'. Arguably more impressive are the children's poems arising from Koch's other method, described in his second book, which involves taking the 'poetry idea' from classic adult poems such as William Blake's 'The Tyger' and presenting it to children in a form they can imitate, for example: 'I asked my students to write a poem in which they were asking questions of a mysterious and beautiful creature' (Koch, 1973: xxii). For Koch, 'a poetry idea should be easy to understand, it should be immediately interesting, and it should bring something new into the children's poems' (Koch, 1970: 14). In Koch's classrooms, poetry writing is often a collaborative activity, in contrast to the highly individual and personal creations of Hughes' young writers.

Given their practical if very different approaches, both Hughes' and Koch's books were influential with classroom teachers in ways that more academic contributions to the poetry teaching debate were probably not. Their impact continued into the 1980s through other popular poetry writing manuals/anthologies that they influenced. Hughes' book inspired the work of middle school teacher Jill Pirrie, whose *On Common Ground* appeared in 1987 with a foreword by Hughes. Pirrie, like Hughes, believed that: 'in so far as all children have memories, all children are embryo poets' (Pirrie, 1987: 6). She made use of more technical exercises and structures than Hughes, but only for the purpose of 'guiding children through the process of writing, while at the same time preserving the freshness and spontaneity which must be the hallmark of their work' (p. 7). In her chapter in this book, Catriona Nicholson writes about the enduring influence of Jill Pirrie on her own very successful classroom practice.

Primary school teacher Sandy Brownjohn's bestselling books, beginning with *Does it Have to Rhyme?* in 1980, were closer in approach to Koch, adding further non-rhyming structures and poetry games to his repertoire. In contrast to the stress on observation and interpretation of personal experience and memories by Hughes and Pirrie, Brownjohn emphasised mastery of form, stating: 'I see the teaching of poetry writing to children as the teaching of skills and techniques almost as much as the use of original ideas ...'. She also justified poetry's place in the curriculum in terms of skills teaching: 'I would almost go as far as to say that most necessary skills in English can be taught through poetry at this [7–14 years] level' (1980: 7).

1970s and 1980s

As Richard Andrews (1991) goes on to show in his survey, the 1970s and 1980s saw the rise of 'process writing' and the 'writer's workshop' approach, developing out of the creative writing movement and its emphasis on process over product. Influential books by American educators led the way here: for example, Donald Graves' *Writing: Children and Teachers at Work* (1983), and Lucy Calkins' *The Art of Teaching Writing* (1986). The processes of writing which were the focus of attention in a writer's workshop might include, for example: getting ideas, conferencing, drafting, editing and publishing. The young writer was seen as needing to go through the same stages of composition and presentation as the professional author. These processes were more important than the actual writing forms, structures or genres used. Any substantial piece of writing could be subject to this process, including poetry, though the emphasis of Graves' work tends to be on sustained narrative writing rather than poems.

As far as poetry reading was concerned, the 1980s also saw the development of reader response approaches and their application in the classroom, which Andy Goodwyn discusses in detail in his chapter. This drew on the work of earlier literary theorists such as Wolfgang Iser (1978) and Louise Rosenblatt (1938, 1978) who attempted to put the reader at the heart of literary studies rather than the text or the author, as in previous critical approaches. In the words of one extreme advocate of reader-centred approaches, Stanley Fish, this involved accepting that: 'Interpretation is not the art of construing but the art of constructing. Interpreters do not decode poems: they make them' (Fish, 1980: 327). Rosenblatt's concept of a transaction between reader and text, where what the reader brings to the text is as important as what is there on the page, was particularly influential, especially since she tended to focus more than Iser on poetry rather than fiction. Rosenblatt stressed the importance of 'aesthetic reading', where readers created meaning from the 'blueprint' or 'stimulus' of the text and thus a multiplicity of possible meanings was available. This was in contrast to what she called 'efferent reading', more common in the poetry classroom, where the reader was directed, usually by the teacher, towards one correct interpretation which could be reproduced for assessment purposes.

Michael and Peter Benton, individually, were leading figures in the practical application of these theories to the classroom through a number of professional and research publications in the second half of the 1980s. Together, they have also produced influential classroom poetry anthologies from the 1960s through to today, such as the *Touchstones* series, and their celebrated trio of anthologies exploring the interplay of poetry and painting, *Double Vision* (1990) *Painting with Words* (1995) and *Picture Poems* (1997), mentioned by Andy Kempe in his chapter in this book. Peter Benton's *Pupil, Teacher, Poem* (1986) presented a survey of secondary teachers' views of poetry teaching, revealing many 'problems and anxieties', even though 'there was still a very high value set on the teaching of poetry' (Benton, 1986: 32). In response to these difficulties, Peter Benton suggested that 'there is a real need to focus less on the teaching of poetry and more on the experience of it', and he put forward 'strategies by which pupils can learn to read poems, to engage with them actively and to talk without teacher domination' (p. 33). Benton provided examples of children using 'lightly-structured, self-directed' group discussion (p. 64) and other active approaches to reading and discussing poems as alternatives to writing about them, for example choral speaking, presentations, group anthologies, videoing, cloze, sequencing, and looking at poets' drafts. The rationale behind these 'response activities' was: 'better that it [poetry] is handled, however roughly, than set apart as a sacred mystery never to be touched and, in consequence maybe, never to touch our pupils' (p. 65). This echoed Auden and Garrett's well-known comment half a century earlier: 'Those ... who try to put poetry on a pedestal only succeed in putting it on the shelf' (Auden and Garrett, 1935: vii). Lionel Warner discusses this enduring problem for poetry teaching at the start of his chapter in this book.

Michael Benton was influential in developing the pedagogy of reader response theory in publications such as *Teaching Literature: Nine to Fourteen* (Benton & Fox, 1985), where he collaborated with Geoff Fox to produce a very popular and practical guide to developing pupil response in the primary as well as secondary classroom. Along with three teacher-researchers, Michael Benton also contributed to *Young Readers Responding to Poems* (Benton et al., 1988) where action research into response activities with KS3 pupils is framed by theoretical discussion of a response-centred methodology for teaching poetry. Patrick Dias and Mike Hayhoe's *Developing Response to Poetry* (1988) continued this effort to translate the insights of literary theory into a coherent and practical teaching approach. How much reader-oriented approaches, such as pupil-directed group discussions, have gone on to gain a foothold in the mainstream of classroom poetry teaching, either at primary or secondary school level, is debatable. The twin constraints of curriculum and assessment demands have tended to marginalise these response-based activities, as Andy Goodwyn's research, quoted in his chapter in this book, suggests (Goodwyn, 2010).

However, developments in response pedagogy did go on to influence national government initiatives in English and in poetry teaching in particular in the late 1980s. *Teaching Poetry in the Secondary School: An HMI View* (DES, 1987), an unusual government monograph published with a pastel-coloured, decoratively lettered cover (a treasure trove for semiotic analysis!), actually presented a very bleak overview of secondary school poetry at the time and endorsed the sort of group response activities promoted by the Bentons and others as the way forward, including performances of poetry and children writing their own poems at secondary school level as well as primary. The first National Curriculum (NC) document, introduced in 1988, incorporated recommended strategies from the reader response-centred pedagogy of the 1980s, as well as the process approaches to writing mentioned earlier. This document was produced under the chairmanship of Brian Cox, a Professor of English but also a published poet. Cox's high regard for poetry within the English curriculum had positive as well as unintentionally negative effects. For the first time, speaking and listening to poetry, and reading it were specifically enshrined as legal entitlements for all pupils in the English curriculum from 5 to 16. However, such was the high value Cox placed on poetry, he did not specifically include writing a poem in either the Programmes of Study or the Attainment Targets for English, arguing that a child should never 'be required to write a poem in order to achieve a particular level of attainment' (Cox, 1991: 147). Although laudable, this over-protective stance has meant that poetry writing, because not specifically assessed, has not been regarded with the same importance as those aspects of the English NC that are assessed. Similarly, the fact that poetry reading rarely appeared in the KS2 National Curriculum Tests (the SATs), and poetry writing never, has perversely diminished their perceived importance by teachers (DES, 1989: 17.29).

The late 1980s also saw a number of important contributions to the debate about how poetry should be taught in schools following the publication of the first NC programmes of study. At almost the same time that the NC became law, three books appeared which in their different ways promoted poetry writing as central to English teaching. George Marsh's *Teaching through Poetry* and Robert Hull's *Behind the Poem*, both published in 1988, stressed the importance of the drafting process and the need to take a longer-term view of children's progress as writers, with its unpredictable outcomes. Both illustrated their arguments with practical teaching suggestions and impressive examples of poetry by primary and secondary age pupils throughout. The poet Michael Rosen's *Did I Hear You Write?* (1989) was a poetry-writing manual and anthology similar in type to the earlier books by Hughes, Koch, Pirrie and Brownjohn, and similarly influential. The approach to poetry writing Rosen advocated, though, was very different, particularly from the methods of Koch and Brownjohn with their emphasis on the use of structures.

Rosen described his own poetry and the work he tried to help children to write as 'memorable speech' (Auden & Garrett, 1935: v). This 'oral writing', reflected in his book's title, involved children using the resources of their own spoken language, community culture and personal experience as the inspiration for flexible free verse poems, rather than literary language or structures which tempted them to be false to their own voices, a danger Ted Hughes had warned of earlier. Rosen presented examples of practical 'starting points for oral writing' and an anthology of children's poems, with notes, to illustrate his approach. In contrast, Linda Hall in *Poetry for Life*, also published in the same year as Rosen's book, complained about the obsession with 'relevance' in poetry teaching and of 'the current practice in primary schools ... to shunt all pupils into the narrow vein and dead end of "free verse" or "chopped-up prose" ... Because some can't rhyme, none shall' (Hall, 1989: 117). She painted a depressing picture of poetry as neglected, disliked or badly taught in both primary and secondary schools; at best an 'optional extra' (p. 3). Hall's complaints about poetry being used as a means to an end as part of a topic, theme or subject, and her call for it to be taught for pleasure and appreciation rather than study, in ways which are less 'threatening' for teachers and pupils and which allow for some stillness and silence, still ring true today. However, her solutions seem unduly restrictive, for example a diet of rhyming, preferably classic poetry, and an end to 'gimmicks' such as background music and sound effects: 'No visual-display material is needed, as poems create their own pictures in the individual mind of the reader' (p. 69). James Carter's chapter in this volume argues persuasively for the importance of the audio-visual in both reading and writing poems, and for poetry that works on the stage as well as the page.

1990s and 2000s

Richard Andrews' *The Problem with Poetry* (1991), already mentioned, entered the post-NC debate about poetry teaching's current state and future prospects with a much more detailed and theoretically informed analysis of what makes poetry problematic, both for teachers and learners, and how these difficulties might be overcome. Andrews also saw his book as 'an attempt to argue for the place of poetry in the curriculum at a time when it seems threatened by more pragmatic and more assessment-driven forms of education' (p. 134). He did this by trying to reconcile what he saw as false oppositions in poetry teaching: for example, between formalism and 'creative writing', between written and oral forms, and between the reading and writing of poetry.

The 1990s saw a revival of interest in teaching rhyming poetry, particularly to very young children, from an unexpected source. Research into early reading and spelling by academics such as Peter Bryant and Usha Goswami (1990) highlighted the importance of exposure to rhyme and alliteration in developing children's phonological awareness, a predictor of later reading and writing attainment. Roger Beard's edited volume *Rhyme, Reading and Writing* (1995) presented different perspectives, from linguistics, psychology and literature, in arguing the case for rhyming poetry, including the cultural heritage case, endorsing Linda Hall's earlier contribution, and criticising the 'sketchy references to rhyme' in the NC documents (p. 20).

The end of the 1990s saw another significant government intervention in English teaching: the National Literacy Strategy (NLS), introduced into primary schools in 1998–99 and later into secondary. Produced in response to a political agenda of raising standards in reading and writing, as measured by the NC tests, this attempt to transform the subject of English into a narrower concept of 'Literacy' had both positive and negative impacts on poetry teaching, just like the NC itself a decade earlier. On the plus side, poetry was now required to be taught in every term in the primary school years, and poetry writing was represented fully alongside poetry reading, although speaking and listening was excluded from this original programme. Less appealing was the level of prescription in the NLS, which involved detailing exactly which type of poetry should be taught each term and providing objectives at text, sentence and word level which needed to be met through each term's teaching. Not only this, but the actual lesson structure to be used was specified: the 'Literacy Hour', divided into timed 'interactive whole class' and ability group activities. The approach to writing generally in the NLS was influenced by 'genre theory', an approach developed by theorists such as the Australians Frances Christie and Pam Gilbert in the 1980s and 1990s which stressed children's need to be taught the structural characteristics of public forms of writing, including poetry. Genre theorists were sceptical about process writing and vague concepts of creativity in writing (see e.g. Christie, 1990: 18–19). Although the NLS was not statutory like the NC, in practice it was almost universally adopted in primary schools as it was the recommended way to meet the NC requirements for reading and writing.

The teacher and poet Dennis Carter was one of the first to engage with the new requirements of the NLS. His book *Teaching Poetry in the Primary School: Perspectives for a New Generation* (1998) was an impassioned attempt to reconcile 'the demands made by poetry, the spirit of creativity and the nature and needs of children' with the NC and NLS, since, he warned, 'unless these contrary forces *are* reconciled ... the future of poetry in schools and, more importantly, the future development of children's sensibilities are grim indeed' (p. 1). Carter felt that the introduction of the NLS was actually an opportunity to develop poetry: 'the highly concentrated focus on literacy in the NLS "Framework" can lead to genuine and strong engagement with poetry in our primary schools' (p. 9). He went on to give detailed suggestions for planning, assessing, reporting and recording poetry in primary schools, including literacy hour lessons for a week for each year group.

In 2000–01, the NLS was extended to Key Stage 3 (11–14 years) with the publication of the *Framework for Teaching English: Years 7, 8 and 9* (DfEE, 2001). As Sue Dymoke has said in her helpful survey of poetry teaching since the introduction of the NC: 'When compared with the detailed list of poetry writing references in the strategy document for Key Stages 1 and 2 (5–11 years), the references to writing in the Framework seem rather thin' (Dymoke, 2003: 16). The same can be said of references to reading poetry in the Teaching Objectives: for example, only one out of nearly 100 objectives for Year 7 referred specifically to reading poems and this was not picked out as one of the 20 key objectives. The *Framework for Teaching English: Years 7, 8 and 9* was revised in 2007, becoming *The Framework for Secondary English*, based on the programmes of study for the new secondary NC of 2008. This 'renewed' *Framework* begins with an encouraging statement about the importance of English taken from the secondary NC:

'Pupils learn to become enthusiastic and critical readers of stories, poetry and drama as well as non-fiction and media texts, gaining access to the pleasure and world of knowledge that reading offers' (DCSF, 2007: 1). However there are no specific references in the learning objectives to reading or writing poetry.

A 'renewed' *Primary Framework for Literacy* for primary schools was also produced in 2006 (DfES, 2006). Speaking and Listening, including group discussion and drama, which had been part of the KS3 *Framework* since its introduction, was now included, encouraging possible links with poetry work. There was a greater emphasis on flexibility in the implementation of what were now 'learning' rather than 'teaching' objectives. Reading independently for pleasure, including poetry, was also an explicit part of the 'Engaging with and Responding to Texts' strand of the *Framework*. However, along with the decreased prescription came a dilution of the poetry requirements: virtually all the specific references to reading and writing poetry term by term in the original NLS were now removed. Although there was an array of online supporting documents giving helpful guidance on 'Progression in Poetry' and providing example poetry units for each year, no longer was poetry's place guaranteed in every term of the primary school (http://nationalstrategies.standards. dcsf.gov.uk/primary/primaryframework).

The NC, 'slimmed down' in 1995, was revised again in 1999, this version retaining specific mention of poetry both in the reading and writing programmes of study right through from KS1 to KS4. However, at the end of the first decade of the new millennium, there was a more radical overhaul of the NC. As mentioned, a new and separate secondary NC was introduced in 2008. The learning objectives here were now generic and made no specific reference to poetry, although the 'range and content' of the programmes of study did specify 'stories, poetry and drama drawn from different historical times, including contemporary writers', 'texts from the English literary heritage', and 'texts from different cultures and traditions', all of which were illustrated with examples of possible poets whose work might be used (QCA, 2007, pp. 70–1). The range of pupils' writing also included poems amongst the different kinds of forms to be used (http://curriculum.qcda.gov.uk). A very different primary NC, with six areas of learning partly replacing the traditional subjects, was due to be introduced into primary schools in 2011. However, at the time of writing, the change of government at the British general election of 2010 has led to the abandonment of this curriculum and the new coalition government's alternative proposals, though promised, have not yet appeared.

Where Are We Now?

Over 20 years since the introduction of the NC in English schools and more than 10 years since the implementation of the National Literacy Strategy, there is now an opportunity for a fresh look at poetry teaching. Recent developments such as the introduction of a more flexible curriculum and the abolition of NC tests at Key Stage 3, confirmation that both the Primary and Secondary Frameworks for Literacy will be withdrawn by 2011, and promised changes to the primary NC mentioned above, make this a good time to take stock of where we are in poetry teaching and to consider what good practice, which does indeed bring poetry alive in the classroom, might look like. If we are approaching a period of increased teacher autonomy, of freedom from centralised prescription and target-setting, when Mr Boon could again succeed Mr Platt in the poetry classroom, this is an ideal opportunity to reclaim what is most effective from the past of poetry teaching, detailed above, as well as to explore new ideas.

Recent reports and research suggest that poetry is an area of English teaching which remains less well developed than others. A report based on Ofsted inspection evidence, *Poetry in Schools: a Survey of Practice 2006–7* (Ofsted, 2007), concluded encouragingly that 'provision for poetry was at least satisfactory in all the schools visited and good or very good in around two-thirds' (p. 4). However, 'it was weaker than the other aspects of English inspected, suggesting that poetry was underdeveloped in many of the schools surveyed' (p. 4). Ofsted's finding that 'many teachers, especially in the primary schools, did not know enough about poetry' (p. 4) and tended to work with a narrow range of poems, has been backed up by other recent research such as the United Kingdom Literacy Association's *Teachers as Readers* project (Cremin et al., 2009).

On the other hand, there have also been high profile initiatives in recent years to raise the status of poetry and poets in school. The 2009 BBC TV competition and subsequent book *Off By Heart* (Goodwin, 2009) helped to revive and publicise the tradition of children learning and reciting a poem. Andrew Motion's 10-year tenure of the Poet Laureateship saw the development of initiatives to bring poets into schools, either virtually or in person, such as The Poetry Archive website (www.poetryarchive.org), the Writing Together scheme (www.writingtogether.org. uk) and Poetryclass, where poets provide in-service training for teachers (www. poetryclass.net). Motion has been succeeded by Carol Ann Duffy, a poet whose work is read in both secondary and primary schools, and who has done much to stimulate interest at KS4 (14–16 years) through her *Poetry Live* performances. Michael Rosen's two years as Children's Laureate, ending in 2009, have seen him champion the 'poetry-friendly classroom', often in the face of the previously mentioned curriculum and assessment pressures which have worked against this. He has emphasised reading aloud and presenting poetry to audiences, and has brought poetry for children and its performance firmly into the age of *YouTube* and other electronic media with his recently launched website *Perform a Poem*, featuring children's own presentations (http://performapoem.lgfl.org.uk).

Bringing Poetry Alive

The contributors to this volume all have many years' experience of bringing together children, teachers and poetry in schools and other settings, either as poets, teachers, teacher trainers, researchers or combinations of these roles. All also have a connection with the University of Reading, as lecturers, external examiners, or current or former graduate students. Lorna, the Reception class teacher featured in the case study in Chapter 2, is also a Reading graduate. They are able to speak with authority about the current 'state of the art' of poetry teaching and about what they feel works best in poetry classrooms in the second decade of the new millennium. They do not all agree on all aspects of poetry teaching; however, they are united in their passionate belief in the centrality of poetry in the school curriculum and in the lives of their students. The purpose of the book is not to instruct readers how to teach poetry in any one particular way, but to inspire the same belief in them and to invite them into dialogue with the various contributors about how poetry can best be taught today. After all, books don't teach poetry; teachers do.

In the first chapter, **Michael Rosen** begins by reflecting on his tenure as Children's Laureate, during which he found many schools lacking any idea of what the point of poetry teaching was, let alone the best way to do it. He describes how he spent much of his Laureateship trying to combat what he calls 'NLS Disease', where poetry was reduced either to an incidental treat or a dutiful chore. He goes on to discuss the initiatives he introduced and has continued to develop to try to counter this situation, and then presents his contribution to what he feels is still a much-needed campaign to recognise the important place poetry should have in schools.

If poetry is to be an important part of children's learning, this needs to happen from the very beginning of primary education. In her chapter, **Margaret Perkins** uses a case study of one highly successful Reception classroom to demonstrate what the teaching of poetry in the early years might look like at its best. She emphasises the need for verbal play with sounds and rhymes in order to 'bed the ear' in Seamus Heaney's phrase (2002: 18); something which continues to be important for children at later stages, as Catriona Nicholson and Andy Kempe show in their chapters.

Perkins' case study also illustrates the importance of the teacher being a reader of poetry, a point taken up by **Prue Goodwin** in her contribution. For Goodwin, the teacher is central to effective poetry teaching; bringing poetry alive requires a teacher who is passionate both about poems and about teaching children, and who can be creative in bringing the two together. In her chapter, she focuses on creative ways of engaging pupils in the later primary years (7–11) with appropriate poems and through response activities involving discussion, exploring language, performance and music-making.

Catriona Nicholson also deals with this important KS2 age-range, where children can often produce their most memorable poetry work, given the right learning environment, but her chapter focuses on writing. Using striking examples of children's own poetry, she demonstrates how the approaches recommended by Jill Pirrie and Ted Hughes can continue to work effectively in the hands of a sympathetic teacher. Like Rosen and Perkins earlier, and James Carter in the next chapter, Nicholson stresses the need for children to be given the freedom to express their own creativity, to retain ownership of their poems, and for their potential achievements not to be underestimated.

James Carter, like Michael Rosen, writes as a visiting poet and therefore offers a different perspective on poetry teaching. He describes in detail the various kinds of visits he makes to schools in the UK and abroad, and reflects on what he encounters there. He also gives advice on what teachers can do to make the most of such opportunities for themselves and for their pupils. It has come to be accepted wisdom that visiting artists are a good thing in the classroom, but Carter tries to provide specific answers to these fundamental questions: 'Why are poets invited into school?' and 'What are "real live" poets good for?'

In her chapter, **Eileen Hyder** confesses to being frustrated as a teacher by those same restrictions imposed by the NLS that Michael Rosen mentions. She describes the sense of release from the confinement of poetry within a narrow Literacy curriculum when she discovered the potential of poetry writing across the curriculum. Presenting examples of children's work which straddle the KS2/3 divide, Hyder convincingly demonstrates how cross-curricular poetry can both consolidate learning in different subject areas and provide meaningful contexts for poems which use a variety of forms. Like Catriona Nicholson, she also stresses the importance of young writers being readers, of the nourishment provided by the 'nectar' of other writers' work.

The teenage years are a period when many pupils struggle to engage with school poetry, however positive they may have been about it earlier. **Lionel Warner** deals with teaching poetry to 11–14 year olds, traditionally the most difficult phase to work in, where surveys repeatedly show that attitudes to poetry become increasingly negative as pupils move through the early secondary school years. He considers this 'groan factor' which can accompany poetry at KS3, but finds on balance a more optimistic picture of how poetry is received by teachers and pupils. Warner also reminds us how teaching poetry at this stage is transitional and looks at the challenges of ensuring progression from KS2 and towards KS4 which the lower secondary teacher must address. He deals with both the reading and writing of poetry with teenagers and, like Eileen Hyder, reflects on productive cross-curricular links for poetry writing which can still be found in the subject-led secondary curriculum.

It is the linkage between poetry and drama which **Andy Kempe** explores in the following chapter, drawing on examples from across the entire primary and secondary school age-range. He argues that, for the dramatising of poems to be most effective, children of all ages need to be made aware of the art form of drama as well as that of poetry. However, he also shows that there needs to be a clear progression in how pupils learn to view a poetic text as a script as they move from simple nursery rhymes to sophisticated literature. Kempe, like earlier contributors, also reflects on the importance of poetry texts such as those of Roger McGough and Michael Rosen, in his own development as a reader and as a teacher.

Finally, **Andy Goodwyn** returns to the problems posed for poetry teachers across all age groups by the constraints of national syllabuses and examinations.

He reflects on the challenges teachers face in cutting through these barriers and getting their pupils to enjoy the emotional charge of poetry, connecting with poems personally through what he calls 'literary reading'. Drawing on his own research, Goodwyn puts forward practical suggestions for how teachers can do this and make the Reader Response classroom a reality, for example by encouraging 'slow reading' and 'creative reading' as an antidote to what can often be a rapid scan through poetry in search of formal features.

References

Andrews, R. (1991) *The Problem with Poetry*. Milton Keynes: Open University Press.

Auden, W.H. & Garrett, J. (1935) 'Introduction', *The Poet's Tongue: An Anthology*. London: G. Bell.

Baldwin, M. (1959) *Poetry without Tears*. London: Routledge & Kegan Paul.

Beard, R. (ed.) (1995) *Rhyme, Reading and Writing*. London: Hodder and Stoughton.

Benton, M. & Benton, P. (1990) *Double Vision*. London: Hodder Arnold.

Benton, M. & Benton, P. (1995) *Painting with Words*. London: Hodder & Stoughton.

Benton, M. & Benton, P. (1997) *Picture Poems*. London: Hodder and Stoughton.

Benton, M. & Fox, G. (1985) *Teaching Literature: Nine to Fourteen*. Oxford: Oxford University Press.

Benton, M., Teasey, J., Bell, R. & Hurst, K. (1988) *Young Readers Responding to Poems*. London: Routledge.

Benton, P. (1986) *Pupil, Teacher, Poem*. London: Hodder and Stoughton.

Bryant, P. and Goswami, U. (1990) *Phonological Skills and Learning to Read*. Hove: Lawrence Erlbaum.

Brownjohn, S. (1980) *Does it Have to Rhyme?* London: Hodder and Stoughton.

Calkins, L. (1986) *The Art of Teaching Writing*. Portsmouth, NH: Heinemann.

Carter, D. (1998) *Teaching Poetry in the Primary School: Perspectives for a New Generation*. London: David Fulton.

Christie, F. (ed.) (1990) *Literacy for a Changing World*. Victoria: Australian Council for Educational Research.

Clegg, A. (1964) *The Excitement of Writing*. London: Chatto & Windus.

Cox, B. (1991) *Cox on Cox: An English Curriculum for the 1990s*. London: Hodder and Stoughton.

Cremin, T., Mottram, M., Collins, F., Powell, S. & Safford, K. (2009) *Teachers as Readers: Building Communities of Readers*. United Kingdom Literacy Association.

Day Lewis, C. (1944) *Poetry for You: A Book for Boys and Girls on the Enjoyment of Poetry*. Oxford: Blackwell.

Department for Children, Schools and Families (DCSF) (2007) *Framework for Secondary English*. London: DCSF.

Department for Education and Employment (DfEE) (2001) *Framework for Teaching English: Years 7, 8 and 9*. London: DfEE.

Department of Education and Science (DES) (1987) *Teaching Poetry in the Secondary School: An HMI View*. London: HMSO.

Department of Education and Science (DES) (1989) *English for Ages 5–16: Proposals of the Secretary of State for Education and Science and the Secretary of State for Wales* (The Cox Report). York: National Curriculum Council.

Department for Education and Skills (DfES) (2006) *Primary Framework for Literacy and Mathematics*. London: DfES.

Dias, P. & Hayhoe, M. (1988) *Developing Response to Poetry*. Milton Keynes: Open University Press.

Dymoke, S. (2003) *Drafting and Assessing Poetry: A Guide for Teachers*. London: PCP.

Fish, S. (1980) *Is There a Text in This Class? The Authority of Interpretive Communities*. Cambridge, MA: Harvard University Press.

Goodwin, D. (ed.) (2009) *Off By Heart: Poems to Learn and Love*. London: Scholastic.

Goodwyn, A. (2010) *The Expert Teacher of English*. London: Routledge.

Graves, D. (1983) *Writing: Children and Teachers at Work*. Portsmouth, NH: Heinemann.

Hall, L. (1989) *Poetry for Life: a Practical Guide to Teaching Poetry in the Primary School*. London: Cassell.

Heaney, S. (2002) *Finders Keepers: Selected Prose 1971–2001*. London: Faber and Faber.

Hourd, M. (1949) *The Education of the Poetic Spirit: A Study in Children's Expression in the English Lesson*. London: Heinemann.

Hughes, T. (1967) *Poetry in the Making: An Anthology of Poems and Programmes from 'Listening and Writing'*. London: Faber and Faber.

Hull, R. (1988) *Behind the Poem: A Teacher's View of Children Writing*. London: Routledge.

Iser, W. (1978) *The Act of Reading: A Theory of Aesthetic Response*. London: Routledge & Kegan Paul.

Koch, K. (1970) *Wishes, Lies and Dreams*. New York: Harper and Row.

Koch, K. (1973) *Rose, Where Did You Get That Red?* New York: Random House.

Marsh, G. (1988) *Teaching through Poetry: Writing and the Drafting Process*. London: Hodder and Stoughton.

Ofsted (2007) *Poetry in Schools: A Survey of Practice 2006–7*. London: Ofsted.

Pirrie, J. (ed.) (1993) *Apple Fire: The Halesworth Middle School Anthology*. Newcastle: Bloodaxe Books.

Qualifications and Curriculum Authority (QCA) (2007) *English Programme of Study for KS3 and Attainment Targets*. London: QCA.

Reeves, J. (1958) *Teaching Poetry: Poetry in Class Five to Fifteen*. London: Heinemann.

Rosen, M. (1989) *Did I Hear You Write?* London: Andre Deutsch.

Rosenblatt, L. (1938) *Literature as Exploration*. New York: Appleton-Century.

Rosenblatt, L. (1978) *The Reader, The Text, The Poem: The Transactional Theory of the Literary Work*. Carbondale, IL: Southern Illinois University Press.

Websites

www.performapoem.lgfl.org.uk
www.poetryarchive.org
www.writingtogether.org.uk

Chapter 1

Reflections on Being Children's Laureate – and Beyond

Michael Rosen

CHAPTER OVERVIEW

In this chapter, Michael Rosen reviews his two-year tenure as Children's Laureate. He describes the worst aspects of the poetry teaching he encountered during his visits to schools and the projects he initiated to try to combat these. He then puts forward his contribution to a manifesto which he feels is needed to argue for the important place of poetry in schools. He concludes his contribution with some detailed practical suggestions for how to approach poetry in the classroom.

What Did I Find?

I'll begin with the worst: I'm going round a school popping into classrooms before doing my show in the hall. The teacher welcomes me in, shows me the class at work and says, 'The Quicks are doing poems and the Slows are doing rhyming words'. For a moment, I'm stunned. I say nothing and move on to the next class, but I'm left wondering how did we get to a situation where it became OK to say in front of a group of children, 'You're the Slows'? And even if there are Slows (which I don't accept), who's to say that these supposed Slows are so slow at poetry that they can't do whole poems? Or that the Quicks are so quick they're ideally suited to do whole poems? Everything I work for in the matter of poetry in schools is underpinned by the idea that it's for everyone – in whatever shape or size, at whatever speed it comes; and whether it's a matter of reading, writing or talking about poems, we shouldn't ever be putting children in a position of being wrong, incompetent, or weak. Doing poetry should be a matter of being right in different ways.

Then, in other schools, over and over again I met National Literacy Strategy Disease. When it came to poetry, this meant slavishly following when, where and how the NLS suggested schools tackle poetry. The consequence of this was that schools were doing haikus when haikus appeared in its particular slot at the given prescribed week in the prescribed term in the prescribed year on the NLS matrix, and only then; same again for narrative poetry, performance poetry and so on through the strange, intermittent, formulaic routine laid down in the Strategy. I saw schools where poetry was ignored for a term and then, in the last week, there was a sudden burst of 'metaphors and similes', unrelated to anything that came before or after, or indeed unrelated to anything very much at all. Over and over again, acrostics seemed to be the standard fall-back position when 'quick 'n easy' results were needed for a display or for a seemingly poetic response to a topic. Meanwhile, there were many classrooms without a poetry corner, with no regular input of the sound of poems, whether that was from recordings or live performances. Many schools seemed to be without any clear sense of what the point of poetry is, what the point of doing it in schools is, or how to do it. I suspect that in the onward rush to score highly in Year 6 SATs, many schools took up the position that the best way to get a Year 6 class doing well in 'Writing' was to drill them in mock SATs papers and worksheets with their dull, pointless extracts, followed by questions about facts, chronology and logic. Poetry in this climate came to be seen as some kind of incidental froth, like end-of-the-day quizzes, or, even worse, a chore done to satisfy the matrix.

I spent a good deal of my time during the Laureateship – and since – trying to figure out how we can break out of this cycle. One area I looked at was the many 'how to do poetry' books that are aimed at teachers. At first glance, these are all very teacher- and child-friendly; full of 'good ideas' and neat, easy, proven ways to get children writing poems. But the more I looked at them (and I'm not going to name names) I saw that there's a common thread running through them: poetry in most of these books is a matter of techniques, systems, tricks and forms. Hardly any of them take as a starting point, feelings, thoughts, ideas, observations and dreams, again, I ask myself, how did we get to this? If we look at the world of poetry and at when it works for us as readers and listeners, it will to a great extent be because it arouses feelings in us, gets us thinking, engages with ideas, gets us to look closely (or look afresh) at something, somebody or a relationship, offers us possibilities, takes us into a dream world ... Why then should we think that the best way to excite and interest children in writing poetry should be to start with techniques and tricks? What's the matter with feelings, ideas, looking closely, looking afresh, and dream worlds? And yet, in the same classroom that might be using one of these poetry-technique books, they might also stop off once a week to do 'Circle Time'. Here, in a fine, democratic way, children and teachers talk about feelings, issues and problems. This time is seen as important for every child. It's considered vital that no child is belittled, or silenced, that the children and adults grow to appreciate one another's weaknesses and strengths, that the matter in hand doesn't necessarily have to have a neat measurable outcome: things may sometimes peter out, at other times they may develop, but if the principles are adhered to, there will be a long-term benefit for everyone. In other words, the ideal environment for poetry! Now, I'm not asking that poetry has to take over Circle Time – though a slot for it wouldn't be out of place. Perhaps what I'm hoping for is that something of Circle Time should be allowed to invade poetry ... but more of that later.

What Did I Do?

So what did I do (and still try to do) to counter some of this? During my time as Laureate, I set up the following projects.

1. Poetry-friendly Classroom Page at *Booktrust*

This is a page on *Booktrust's* website aimed directly at teachers (http://www.booktrust.org.uk/Resources-for-schools/Poetry-Friendly-Classroom). On the page, both in video and in print, I've made suggestions as to how to create a poetry-friendly classroom. I've also put a shortened version of this on my own website (http://www.michaelrosen.co.uk). On the page I've asked that, first and foremost, we need to give poetry a home in classrooms and schools, without worrying too much about how to teach it. Our main concern as teachers, educators or poets in schools should be to help children feel comfortable browsing around poems, to not feel threatened by strange or unusual poetry; to help children build up a 'repertoire' of poems that they know. This means coming up with many varied ways of presenting poetry, of encouraging children to read it, hear it, view it and make it their own. What I've offered on this webpage is not meant as a blueprint, simply suggestions that teachers can adapt, change and make their own. There's a forum on the page for teachers to talk about their own experiences of teaching poetry.

When it comes to teaching poetry in some kind of formal way, I make the plea that if you're going to ask children questions about poems, then we should all think of ways of shaping these into the kinds of questions that we don't know the answers to. Questions like:

- Does anything in this poem remind you of anything that has ever happened to you, or happened to anyone you've ever heard of? Why or how is that?

- Does anything in this poem remind you of anything you've ever read before, or seen on TV, at the cinema, on the internet? Why or how is that?
- If you could ask anyone or anything in the poem a question, what would you ask?
- If you could ask the author or publisher of the poem any questions, what would you ask?

As a class or in pairs or groups, the children can have a go at answering those questions, perhaps 'in role'.

I think if these kinds of questions are discussed in an open, humane way, involving everyone, taking everything that everyone says seriously (Circle Time ethics, if you like), then the class will get to make deep contact with the poem and will discover that poetry can matter.

When it comes to 'technique', I've expressed the view that in education, we fetishise this. We kid ourselves that if we have children spotting metaphors and alliteration, then something 'real' or 'rigorous' is being taught. But it is only kidding. What's more, I think that there is something pointless about disconnecting 'technique' from what poetic technique (prosody) exists for in the first place. So how should we tackle this? Poetry is a highly specific example of 'cohesion' – that's to say, a way (or really, many ways) of making language 'stick together'. All language sticks words together. If it didn't, it would be gobbledegook. If you look at this paragraph you're reading, you can see several ways in which words and phrases are linked to each other with what is in essence a kind of invisible grammar. In the first sentence of this paragraph, I end on the word 'this'. That 'refers' back (i.e. links back) to something earlier. Also, in that sentence, I use the word 'we'. This stands in for a group of people who aren't visible but it's one way for this passage to reach out to (link with) language beyond this page. The fourth sentence begins with the phrase 'what's more' – which, through the use of the word 'more', links what's coming next to what's just been. It alerts us to the fact that something similar is going to be introduced.

Poetry uses this secret grammar but has other invisible ways of linking words and phrases together. It's quite possible to tell children what some of these are (e.g. rhythm, rhyme, alliteration, repeated images, framing devices, verse structures and patterns and so on), and then ask them to spot these. However, I'm not sure of the educational value of such a process. It involves very little original investigation, discovery or invention. Instead of this process, we can say to children that poetry has 'secret strings' (or something like that), strings that run between words, phrases and letters. We can be 'poem detectives' and hunt for the secret strings. Of course, as a teacher you can make suggestions, but the objective should be to get the maximum amount of investigation, discovery and invention going on.

Then, when, let's say, photocopied poems have been scribbled on, with lines linking all sorts of sounds, words and images, we can ask, what shall we call these lines? Some of them do have names – alliteration and the like – but others don't. Why not encourage the class to make up their own names?

2. *Twinkle Twinkle Little Bat! 250 Years of Poetry for Children*

This was the name of the exhibition that Morag Styles and I curated at the British Library in 2009. It told and demonstrated the history of children's poetry in Britain. The Faculty of Education, Cambridge, produced a DVD of the exhibition so that there is a permanent record of it. In tandem with this, Morag Styles and The Faculty of Education organised a conference on 'Poetry and Childhood' at the British Library (http://www.educ.cam.ac.uk/events/conferences/poetrychildhood), and all the major contributions at the conference appear in a book with the same title (Styles et al., 2010).

It did occur to me that it's possible for colleges, libraries, schools and even single classes to do versions of this. So, if a class has become interested and enthusiastic about poetry, it would be possible to do a poetry project, trying to get some sense of what kind of poems were written across time and across cultures. Poetry for children has a history and it's a history that could easily find a home in classrooms and libraries.

3. *Perform-a-Poem*

As I was thinking of projects to work on in the Laureateship, my son Joe, who is a film-maker, suggested that it would be a good idea for children to have a kind of poetry *YouTube*. In the end, it wasn't possible to create a nationwide site, but with the enthusiastic participation of the London Grid for Learning, we have got an e-safe children's poetry website up and running (http://performapoem.lgfl.org.uk). At the moment, it's only fully available to schools in the London Grid, but there's a limited version available for others to view. In essence, it's a site where schools can upload children's poetry performances, or poetry films, animations and videos.

4. The Philippa Pearce Lecture, the British Library Conference Lecture and the Laureate Lecture

During the Laureateship, it was my job to engage in polemic around poetry and these three lectures provided a context for that. All can be accessed online. The Philippa Pearce Lecture is in Write4Children. (volume 1, issue 2), the Winchester University online journal (http://www.winchester.ac.uk/academic departments/EnglishCreativeWritingandAmericanStudies/publications/write4children/Pages/Write4Children.aspx); the British Library lecture appears in the 'Poetry and Childhood' conference book mentioned above (Styles et al., 2010) and, along with the Laureate lecture 'What is a bong-tree?', is on my website (www.michaelrosen.co.uk).

5. Live Performances

Throughout the Laureateship I carried on doing live poetry performances in schools, theatres, literature festivals and libraries. I try to do about two or three of these a week over the school year. One important way of discovering and enjoying poetry is to hear it and to see poets reading or performing it. This makes for an experience that is a heightened form of what all face-to-face experiences are: a live moment where exchanges of feelings, sensations, ideas and personalities take place. A live show can be a place where questions can be asked, where an audience can feel how they are shaping what's being said by the performer, and something of the thinking and writing processes of a poet can be laid out before them. I've always thought that my job is to both write and perform poetry and that the one isn't more important than the other. I'm pretty sure that over the years, I've reached more children through the live performances than I have with the books. I also hope that these per-formances encourage schools to set up time and space for children's own poetry performances.

6. Course at the Centre for Literacy in Primary Education (CLPE)

I helped run a year-long poetry course for teachers at the CLPE. The first of these became the book, *A Year with Poetry*, that I co-edited with Myra Barrs in 1997. The idea behind the course is that teachers come in to the Centre and experiment then and there with writing poems and coming up with teaching ideas. They share them and then try things out in the classroom over the year and finish with a presentation for each other and for their headteachers and/or their Literacy Postholders at the end of the year. It's a process that could be replicated in teachers' centres and professional development centres everywhere.

7. *Can I Have a Word?*

I continued this project that started in 2004 at the Barbican Centre, London. Local Year 5 children come in to the Centre and work with several poets on projects which either involve exhibits at the Centre (e.g. art exhibitions) or special activities which are set up (e.g. film shows, concerts). The form of the work for the schools involves one day in the autumn term, one day in the spring and some kind of concert in the summer term. The days are a balance between working as a single class with a poet on the exhibit or activity, sharing work with the other five or so schools attending, and listening to the poets' own specially commissioned poems they've written in response to the exhibition or activity. The overall result is a rich and fertile year, with introductions to art, photography, installations, films or music, with poetry acting as a partner and interpreter of these other art forms. It has served as a reminder that poetry is an excellent partner to the other arts. Several thousand London children have had this experience so far. I would hope that other arts centres, museums, galleries, heritage sites and the like could imitate what the Barbican Centre has done here.

8. *Literacy Evolve*

I've acted as a consultant on the *Literacy Evolve* project by Pearson Education (Lockwood, 2009a, b, c, d) to put whole books back at the heart of classrooms. My contribution on the poetry front was to suggest that their collections of poems could take the form of poetry selections presented by the poets themselves. So the poetry selections are not anthologies of several poets, but the selected poems of single poets who 'talk' to the reader in speech bubbles and commentaries. This is an attempt to connect poets to their poems. This technique could be imitated in the way that schools reproduce the children's poems.

Through these eight initiatives, most of which are still up and running, I've tried to counter and challenge the dreary, mechanistic approach to poetry that the NLS imposed on schools.

What More Needs Doing?

It seems to me that we need a manifesto to campaign for the recognition of the importance of poetry in schools, but there's little point in doing this if it is to repeat the mistakes of the National Literacy Strategy. Here's my contribution to such a manifesto:

1. Poetry has a great role to play in education for many reasons:
   (a) It tackles matters of great importance to our emotional lives and it does this in exciting, intriguing and accessible ways.
   (b) It expresses who we are, what we've been and what we might be, and education should in part be about helping pupils do this too.
   (c) It expresses at different times or at the same time: highly individual experiences, culturally specific experiences and common shared experiences, and in so doing can affirm and broaden readers' lives.
   (d) It frequently asks questions, suggests thoughts, offers possibilities and tackles ideas. It often does this without closing off the matter in hand, or wrapping things up with neat conclusions. As a consequence, poetry leaves gaps for readers' thinking and opens up many areas for thought and discussion.

(e) Through its more musical forms it gives children a way of grasping and learning the sound of written language, and it can easily imitate the sound and shape of speech, so making it a perfect bridge between the oral and the written codes.

(f) Because poetry comes in a wide range of forms, many of which are experimental, it shows children that language is flexible, changeable and malleable.

(g) Reading poetry often seems to stimulate people of all ages to want to write it.

2. For such benefits to be available for all children, then poetry teaching has to be itself flexible. There has to be an emphasis on open-ended browsing, reading, listening, viewing, writing, performing and publishing. Tying poems down to right and wrong answers, or prescribing right and wrong ways of reading, performing, listening and writing is counter-productive.

SOMETHING TO THINK ABOUT

It seems to me that many people (probably not those who are reading this book) are anxious about poetry. One of the reasons for this is that the poetry lessons we had at school may have focused on what we didn't know or understand. The teacher, or someone cleverer than us, appeared to know more and understand more. So we ended up sitting in front of a poem, our minds filled with a sense of mild humiliation. Given that this was linked to the exam system, for many of us it turned poetry into a source of anxiety. If, then, we are required to teach poetry, there can easily be a sad, knock-on effect whereby we do the same thing to the children we teach. When I look at the NLS documents, I see and hear that same anxiety: a felt obligation that there are some 'basics' or 'essentials' about poetry that have to be taught and that these can be laid down chronologically as a course; that there are right ways to read poems and these mostly consist of spotting poetic techniques and explaining why they are 'effective'. If we are to make any advances in poetry teaching, where poetry works for a majority of our pupils, we have to break this cycle.

SOMETHING TO READ

Red, Cherry Red (2007), Jackie Kay's fourth poetry collection for children, which comes in the form of an attractively illustrated book, complete with a CD of her introducing and reading the poems. This little book gives readers of all ages access to an engaging and original poetic voice.

SOMETHING TO DO

1. Your main resources for writing poetry are:

   - **Feelings** (what feelings feel like)
   - **Reminiscences** (memory, recall of moments in your life, the 'photo album' of your personal history)
   - **The need to say something to somebody**
   - **Dreams and day-dreams**
   - **Hopes** (expressing wishes and desires, for yourself, for others, for your area, for your 'people', for society, for the world)
   - **Word-play** (sound, nonsense, musicality of language)
   - **Other poems** (as triggers for thought and ideas about what is possible to say in poetic ways)
   - **Other forms of literature and entertainment** (fiction, films, TV, etc.)
   - **Talk** (sharing stories, thoughts and feelings)
   - **Activity** (trips, outings, classroom work, making things, doing things, playing)
   - **Reflection** (describing and thinking about something around you)
   - **Suggestion** (not saying exactly what something is, just giving a hint)
   - **Ventriloquism** (speaking in someone else's voice, or in the imagined voice of a thing – a toy, a school, someone in a story, or even in the voice of an idea or feeling like 'Love' or 'Anger')
   - **Stream of consciousness** (doing a running commentary of what is going on in your mind as you are doing something)
   - **Catch-phrases** (clichés, proverbs, idioms, axioms, repeated statements, instructions, dictums, homilies, commands, slogans, lines from songs and poems, famous sayings, quotes)
   - **Comparison** (how one thing is like another, how one thing can represent another, for example in metaphor, simile and symbol)
   - **Argument and dispute** (representing disagreement between people or ideas)
   - **Image** (looking at pictures, paintings, photos, sculptures and figuring out what people or things in the image are thinking, saying, seeing, imagining, wondering)
   - **Music** (listening to music and writing down what you're thinking)
   - **Identity** (what it means to be me)
   - **Culture** (what it means to be 'us' – however defined; what is specific to the kind of people 'we' are)

   Don't think of these as separate. They overlap with each other.

2. At the heart of poetry are poets writing poems about: what they **see**, what they **hear**, what they **feel**, what they **touch**, what they hear people (including themselves) **saying**, what they **imagine** other people are **thinking**, what they **imagine** could or might happen.

(Continued)

(Continued)

3. Take these ideas of seeing, hearing, feeling, touching, saying, thinking and imagining and see if you can apply them to any of the list of 'resources' above.

So, for example, take 'talk' and 'reminiscence':

- You set the children up in pairs to reminisce about a moment when they were scared (or any other moment in their lives that you think matters to them).
- You might want to use a film, a poem or a story as a trigger for this talk.
- Ask them to think about and then talk about what they could see, hear, feel and think in their moment of fear.
- What were people (including themselves) saying and imagining?
- Ask the children to jot these thoughts down as answers to questions such as: What could you see? What could you hear?
- At this point you could write a class poem by making a montage of answers, taking contributions from everyone, no matter how brief.
- Say that the children's job is to turn their own jottings into a piece of writing that will give the person reading it the feeling that they are there with you at that moment, seeing what you saw, feeling what you felt, imagining what you imagined.
- Say that this is not a story. They should be just trying to 'give the impression' or the feeling of what it was like. It doesn't have to be whole sentences.
- Share the writing in the class.
- 'Publish' it, by putting it up on the wall or making an 'our scary moments' booklet or a PowerPoint display with images and recordings.
- Get the children to find some poems by published poets that deal with fear and scary moments.
- Share these in a 'poetry show', combining the children's poems with the published poets' poems.

4. Go back to my list of 'resources', and what I've called the 'heart of poetry' above, and make up other combinations, for example:

- 'ventriloquism' and 'argument': a conversation between a playground swing and a slide about who is the best
- 'culture': how do my grandparents speak? What are their favourite expressions? What have they told me that they think is important?
- 'stream of consciousness' and 'dreams': write a running commentary on a dream you've had. In other words, imagine you're a radio

commentator describing yourself in the dream, as it is happening, for example: 'I walk into the room ...'

- 'catch-phrases' and 'word-play': can you collect the school's catch-phrases and play with them by swapping words over from one phrase to another, or cutting words out? (e.g. 'Don't eat the corridors'; 'Be kind to the dinner-hall'...)

5. Find poems by published poets that show similar ways of writing to the ones that the children are writing, so that the children can compare their writing with the poets' writing.
6. Use this list flexibly; make up your own combinations. Find poems that help you do this. Use the poems the children have written to trigger new poems. Display, record and perform as much as you can. Get the children to make their own anthologies and collections of poems. Make handwritten poem posters and put them up on the wall.

References

Barrs, M. & Rosen, M. (1997) *A Year with Poetry: Teachers Write about Teaching Poetry*. London: Centre for Language in Primary Education.

Kay, J. (2007) *Red, Cherry Red*. London: Bloomsbury.

Lockwood, M. (ed.) (2009a) *Literacy Evolve Year 3: Gina Douthwaite and Roger McGough, Collected Poems*. Harlow: Pearson Education.

Lockwood, M. (ed.) (2009b) *Literacy Evolve Year 4: James Carter and Grace Nichols, Collected Poems*. Harlow: Pearson Education.

Lockwood, M. (ed.) (2009c) *Literacy Evolve Year 5: Charles Causley and Michael Rosen, Collected Poems*. Harlow: Pearson Education.

Lockwood, M. (ed.) (2009d) *Literacy Evolve Year 6: Benjamin Zephaniah and Ted Hughes, Collected Poems*. Harlow: Pearson Education.

Styles, M., Joy, L. & Whitley, D. (2010) *Poetry and Childhood*. Stoke-on Trent: Trentham Books.

Websites

http://www.booktrust.org.uk/Resources-for-schools/Poetry-Friendly-Classroom

http://www.educ.cam.ac.uk/events/conferences/poetrychildhood

http://www.michaelrosen.co.uk

http://performapoem.lgfl.org.uk

http://www.winchester.ac.uk/academicdepartments/EnglishCreativeWritingandAmerican Studies/publications/write4children/Pages/Write4Children.aspx

Chapter 2

Teaching Poetry in the Early Years

Margaret Perkins

CHAPTER OVERVIEW

In this chapter, Margaret Perkins begins by establishing the key features of poetry itself and of poetry in the early years of schooling. She then presents a case study of how poetry is taught and learnt in one Reception class (ages 4–5 years), in this way demonstrating what excellent practice might look like. Poetry for listening to, for performing, for word-play, for responding and for writing are all covered. The chapter ends with advice on 'where do I start in teaching poetry?'

I recently visited a friend and spent some time playing with her 5-month-old son, Samuel. He sat on my knee as I bounced him up and down and sang 'Humpty Dumpty' to him. He laughed as he 'fell' off my knee when Humpty Dumpty fell off the wall and very soon came to anticipate the fall. The following day I observed Samuel with his childminder. She too sang traditional songs with him and he laughed and joined in the actions. The difference was that those songs were in French. Samuel lives in Paris and has an English mother and a French father. He is brought up surrounded by both languages and in both of them he was enjoying the rhythm, the sound, the repetition, the pattern and the interaction as he laughed and became involved with the different songs. Is this the beginning of poetry with very young children? If so, what is the relationship between the sound and rhythm of the language and understanding of the meaning? How does this impact on the response made by the listener and/or reader?

In order to understand fully the place poetry plays in the early years setting, I want first to explore at a very basic level what it is we mean by poetry in the early years and also to look at the place it holds in the curriculum. This will then be followed by a case study of one Reception class teacher discussing and describing the role poetry plays in her classroom.

Definitions of Poetry

There are as many definitions of poetry as there are poems and in some senses to define poetry is to limit and restrict it. All definitions relate poetry to the emotions – it is both an expression of and an evocation of deep feeling. For example, Wordsworth is said to have defined poetry as 'the spontaneous over-flow of powerful feelings'. A synthesis of the many definitions to be found would seem to describe poetry as the awareness in the imagination of experiences which are expressed through meaning, sound and language and which evoke an emotional response. Dylan Thomas said of poetry:

> You can tear a poem apart to see what makes it tick … You're back with the mystery of having been moved by words. The best craftsmanship always leaves holes and gaps … so that something that is *not* in the poem can creep, crawl, flash or thunder in. (1961: 45)

It is this we must remember when working with very young children. Poetry is not primarily a teaching tool, although much can be learned through it. Ofsted saw an overemphasis on poetry as a teaching tool as in fact diminishing the power of poetry: 'poetry becomes primarily a teaching tool for language development rather than a medium for exploring experience' (2007:11).

Poetry is not part of the syllabus for phonics although rhyme, rhythm and sound can be learned through it; it is not a means for learning about word classes, metaphors and synonyms, although the right word in the right place is an important element of an effective poem. The main aim of poetry with young children is, in my opinion, to give them those imaginary experiences and the means through which they can express them and explore them further.

Poetry in the Early Years

There can be no discussion of poetry in the early years without an emphasis on the importance of nursery rhymes. In a recent television interview, Philip Pullman said that if he were in government he would want to be 'Minister of

Nursery Rhymes' (*Breakfast*, BBC TV, 14 April 2010). What is it about nursery rhymes that makes them so important for young children? When we look closely at many of them they relate very strange and not very pleasant tales – a farmer's wife cutting off the tails of blind mice, Humpty Dumpty unable to be repaired after his fall, and a blackbird pecking off a maid's nose. Strange, often violent and frequently obscure, these rhymes provide an entry to emotions such as fear, excitement, anticipation, despair, joy, and as such they are powerful introductions to the world of poetry.

Why is it commonly agreed that nursery rhymes are a basic ingredient in the early years? Research is clear on the value that nursery rhymes bring to the literacy development of young children. Knowledge of them sensitizes children to the phonological structure of language, which in turn enhances early reading achievement (Bryant and Bradley, 1985; Bryant and Goswami, 1990). Nursery rhymes also provide strong social and cultural links (Brice Heath, 1983). It is important to remember that there will be children in classes who know rhymes from different cultures and in different languages. These rhymes are equally valuable for attuning the ear to the sounds and rhythms of language, and the stories establish and value different cultural heritages.

Nursery rhymes contain strong rhythm and rhyme. There is usually a strong narrative element and it is possible for the reader to engage with the rhyme through action. And within the definitions established earlier it can certainly be claimed that nursery rhymes are poetry; they evoke emotional responses to imaginative experiences in the minds of young children. Bruce and Spratt (2008) argue that nursery rhymes are part of the canon of literature which connects with the traditions of culture. They also encourage a sensitivity to the rhythms and sound patterns of language.

A quick scan of the indexes of recent books published on early years language shows that poetry does not appear very often. However, rhyme does. It is interesting to note that, for many early years practitioners, poetry is seen as the 'bridge into phonic work' (Bruce and Spratt, 2008: 120) and is given its place in the curriculum as a part of phonological awareness. However, Whitehead (2010) does include poetry in the index of her book, *Language and Literacy in the Early Years*, and argues that 'play with the material of language is the art of poetry' (2010: 24). The entries in the index about rhyme focus on alliteration, rhythm and rhyme. Rhyme is seen as a natural part of the process of language acquisition and the implication is that it is a necessary precursor to poetry. In the early years, children experience rhyme so that they can progress to poetry later.

The Early Years Foundation Stage Curriculum (DCSF, 2008) includes the term poetry in its final objective for children aged 40–60 months. It describes the text types of stories, rhymes, songs, poems or jingles. It requires children to listen, to have their favourite texts and to explore and experiment with sounds, words and texts. These requirements come under the theme of Communication, Language and Literacy, within the foci of Linking Sounds and Letters and

Reading. The Creative Development theme does not mention poetry. There is no indication of what is meant by poems, in contrast to rhymes.

The *Primary Framework for Literacy* (DfES, 2006) has three units on poetry in each of Year 1 and Year 2. It also has a paper, *Support for Writing* (DCSF, 2008), which defines poetry and this includes the statement: 'As children become familiar with a wider range of poetic forms and language techniques they can make increasingly effective use of wordplay to explore and develop ideas through poetry'.

I want to explore how poetry is an integral part of children's experience in one Reception classroom and to show that this statement is too minimalist in its expectation of the power of poetry in the education of young children. I hope that I can demonstrate how much poetry can indeed do for very young children.

A Case Study

The class is part of a large primary school in a London suburb. There are two parallel Reception classes and Lorna is the teacher in one of those. She is an experienced primary teacher, an Advanced Skills teacher, who is an English specialist and has a passion for poetry. In describing her own attitude towards poetry, she talked about the childhood associations and described poetry as being 'awash with emotions and connotations'. She remembers the teacher reading aloud poetry to her in school and feeling soothed by the language; for Lorna poetry brings security and comfort. She particularly referred to the poetry of Robert Louis Stevenson which was a childhood favourite of hers. The *Teachers as Readers* research (Cremin et al., 2009) emphasised the importance of teachers' own reading experiences and knowledge of texts and this is also true of poetry. Lorna's success as a teacher of poetry with young children undoubtedly comes from her own love and knowledge of poetry. It is this that enables her to bring poetry alive within her classroom. There are several aspects to her work which achieve this aim.

Poetry for Listening To

I introduce poems as things to be listened to – before lunch, at spare moments during the day. I read poetry often – in the odd five minutes. The children will normally hear three to four poems a day.

Poetry is part of the planned read-aloud programme of the class. It is read initially just for the sheer pleasure of hearing the language and the rhythm of the words. Poetry is a strong part of the children's literacy experiences within school. It is read for pleasure and teacher and children together share enjoyment in the poems.

Poems are always freely available in the classroom:

I have a special basket which contains poems – an anthology of poems which are my favourites. I have a Polly Pig which has pockets containing poems – nursery rhymes and songs are the starting point.

There is a clear sense of progression in Lorna's planned reading of poetry. Firstly, she wants to engage the children, to make poetry fun and accessible:

I start with funny poems – tongue twisters with lots of alliteration. The humour attracts the children's attention and tunes them in to the sound of the language. The poems include nonsense poems.

Poems in this category include 'On the Ning, Nang, Nong' by Spike Milligan (1997), 'The Pobble Who Had No Toes' by Edward Lear (1947) and 'Eletelephony' by Laura Richards (1902):

Once there was an elephant,

Who tried to use the telephant—

No! no! I mean an elephone

Who tried to use the telephone

These poems are chosen for their emphasis on fun and playing with language. At this stage for Lorna the understanding does not matter – what does matter is the pleasure the children get from playing with the language. There is a serious point to this too, however. As they play with the language, the children are learning that language is something that they can use, they can manipulate language to do what they want with it; they are in control. Playing with the sounds shows the children how language works, the sound combinations that are normal in English and those that are unusual, and gives them practice in articulation and control over the sounds they themselves can make. There is another benefit; Lorna works in a class where several languages are spoken and in addition to this there are several children with identified special needs. All children in the class can be included in hearing the poems being read. Meaning does not matter; everybody can listen to and make silly sounds and laugh at the results:

It is inclusive – everybody can join in. Children with English as an additional language can join in – there is nothing to stop their participation with the language – it is silly sounds – nobody understands what it means because it's nonsense. We are playing with the sounds of language.

This emphasis on the sound and rhythm of the language continues as Lorna begins to introduce more challenging poetry. These are shared at odd moments during the day. It does not matter to Lorna that the children do not understand all that a poem is about; what does matter is that they experience the poem.

They hear and, perhaps more importantly, feel the sounds, rhythms and emotions. I talked to a 5-year-old girl in Lorna's class who had learned and recited the poem 'The Owl and the Pussy Cat', asking her what her favourite bit was. She repeated the line, 'How charmingly sweet you sing'. When asked why this was her favourite she replied, 'Because it sounds good and is nice to say – it feels lovely in your mouth when you say it'. This is what Lorna means when she says she wants the children to experience poetry. Their experience of poetry can be compared to their experience of the sand, water or construction materials. They are using it to find out what language can do and what they can do with it.

Lorna then goes on to read to the children other more challenging poems – 'A Smuggler's Song' by Rudyard Kipling (1906), 'From a Railway Carriage' by Robert Louis Stevenson (1885) and 'The Highwayman' by Alfred Noyes (1999). They don't understand what these poems mean but they enjoy the sound of the words and the rhythm and they join in with the refrain. It is strongly emphasised that poetry does not have to rhyme. It is the rhythm and the choice of words that is important.

For Lorna the essence of poetry is that it is a 'short sharp burst of rich language'. Poetry is shorter than many other types of texts and has more focus on the language. For children, the pleasure and joy of saying and hearing language – the carefully selected words – gives them an experience of seeing what language can do to and for them and what they can do with language. For young children with a limited concentration span that short, sharp burst of rich language can show them the potential of language.

▬ Poetry for Performing

For Lorna, reading poetry aloud is often a performance:

> I will read poems like 'Albert and the Lion'. I will wear a cap and use an appropriate accent to show the children we don't all talk in the same way – differences are good and to be celebrated and enjoyed.

This shows the children that listening to poetry is not a passive experience but demands an active involvement. This may be just joining in with the teacher but it often means much more than that. Lorna collects bottle tops and tapes them to the bottom of children's shoes. The class goes out to the playground or in the corridor and tap dances to the rhythm of the poems or rhyming stories that are being read. Try it as you read aloud the book *Rap-a-tap-tap* (Dillon & Dillon, 2002), the story of the great tap dancer Mr Bojangles!

A similar activity can be done with the book *Tanka Tanka Skunk* (2003) by Steve Webb. Use musical instruments or experiment with making sounds with different body parts and work out which sound is most appropriate for each animal. Try and make that sound with the syllabic pattern of the words and put the whole together to make a wonderful sound picture of the book as it is read. If you want to be rather more sedate, let the children make marks on a long sheet of paper as the poem is read and later let them construct a symbol to represent a rhyming sound. The children are learning about symbolic representation, are creating their own musical notation, and are really listening to the sound and rhythm of the poem.

Lorna had read her children the poem 'The Owl and the Pussy Cat' by Edward Lear (1871). Carys took this poem to heart. She searched for it on the internet and printed a copy off. She learned the poem by heart and recited it frequently to anybody who would listen. She conscripted a friend and they made masks for an owl, a cat and a pig. They performed it to the whole class who were then put into groups by Lorna and gave a choral performance of the poem. Carys and a group of friends then practised the poem while working out signs or actions to go with the words and again performed it.

After this Lorna talked with the class about the performance. They talked about what they liked and which performance they preferred and why. They discussed in talk partners their responses to the questions, 'How could we improve this performance? What could we make, add or bring to this that would make it better?' Answers from the children included such things as:

- make a puppet show
- wear costumes
- dance to it
- take the words home to show your mum and dad
- perform it to lots more people
- print the words out so people could see it as well as hear it.

Lorna responded positively to all these suggestions and finished the lesson by saying: 'This is ours. This poem now belongs to us. We can take it and make it really special. That's what the poet wants. He gave it to us and so it's ours'.

Poetry for Word-Play

The boys in Lorna's class love poetry too. She thinks it is because poetry is precise and the words are things which are chosen carefully and assembled with thought. Constructing a poem is like working in the construction area with interlocking bricks. The bricks can be fitted together in many different ways, but in order to make your construction match the idea you have in your head you must try lots of different ways: putting together, taking apart and considering the overall effect. So it is with words and poetry. It is personal and so you cannot be wrong. It need not matter about punctuation or grammar – for young children it's just about choosing the right words. As Lorna puts it:

Boys love poetry – they can handle it, it is precise, they can't be wrong, it is personal, it is like construction – fitting words together. There is only one word to consider – they are receptive to the language and don't have to worry about structure and transcription. It is a window of opportunity for listening to and talking about language. They can take in and absorb a poem – it is an opportunity to use and explore language without the constraint of writing a story.

What happens in Lorna's classroom that gives children this delight in language? After hearing poems several times, the children are asked to identify words they like. The class enjoys saying the words together and talking about what they might mean. *What does it make you think of?* Lorna might take a word and each member of the class would say what it means to them, for example, 'Jabberwocky'. *What is it?* Adults and children alike can join in. I was in the classroom once and was discussing the new *Alice in Wonderland* film with Lorna. I said I did not recognise the 'Jabberwock' figure from my own imaginative picture but Lorna did; some children listened and joined in with their images of the Jabberwock and then the teaching assistant joined in. We found the image from the film on the internet and brought it up on the whiteboard; we re-read Lewis Carroll's (1872) description and compared it with the visual image and our own imaginations. Some children went away to draw the Jabberwock; others carried on talking with Lorna about different words to describe it.

Some of these words were displayed on the wall as 'Wow' words. Lorna tells the children that 'Wow' words are words that are exciting, that make you smile, that you are proud to say and that would make adults fall over in amazement. The children write them to put on the wall – often in emergent writing. The classroom is one where language is celebrated.

Poetry for Responding To

Lie down, close your eyes and make pictures in your head. The poet has chosen the words carefully to help you to make pictures in your head.

Lorna puts a big emphasis on the children's own imaginative and personal response to poetry and the instructions above are often to be heard in her classroom. They come after reading a variety of poems to the children, some of which one would not normally expect to hear in a Reception class. For example:

- 'Figgie Hobbin' by Charles Causley (1970)
- 'maggie and milly and molly and may' by E. E. Cummings (1994)
- 'Daffodils' by William Wordsworth (1815)

Lorna asks the children to listen to these poems, to create pictures in their heads and then sometimes, but only sometimes, to transfer those pictures onto paper in whatever medium the children choose.

I don't think there is such a thing as age-appropriate poems – it's the language. It's about developing the imagination, taking them beyond themselves. Children learn it's OK to have an imagination. There is no right or wrong. The words are carefully chosen to have meaning for you – the reader – and to create moods.

The poems used are chosen for their power to stimulate the imagination and the emotions – for that surely is the essence of poetry. The first response to a poem is to imagine and to feel. The emotional and imaginative response comes before the understanding and makes the understanding personal and deeply experienced:

I sing to them a lot – it helps them feel and hear the rhythm and beat. EAL [English as an Additional Language] children will sing a response to the register when they can't say it. Why? The rhythm supports the language.

The integration of music with poetry emphasises both the rhythm and the sound but also the 'feel' of the language. Lorna describes how children in her class who have English as an additional language are able to respond in song when they might not be able to respond in speech; the rhythm and the melody and the language provide a scaffold for their response. The old joke about the child who could sing the tune to the times tables but did not know the words works because it is essentially true. Poetry is the same – the rhythm and the emotion provide the gateway to the language:

Children will perform and recite poetry. They are much more confident in doing this than recounting their news. Poetry gives them confidence because they become immersed in it – it provides a scaffold for their talk. It is the way in to speaking – inclusive.

Poetry for Writing

It has become clear that in Lorna's classroom experience is at the heart of work with poetry and this applies also to writing poetry. In the first half of the Autumn Term she will take the children out into a field to see, hear, touch, smell and taste the growing harvest. They will talk about what they are experiencing and the adults will record in writing the words they use. Back in the classroom they will listen to their own words and refine them and order them so that, in the children's view, they are a powerful representation of the experience they have had.

The same process is applied to other experiences – sweets, bread, snow, rain, materials, toys, and so on. There is a freedom in writing poetry which is not confined by structure. The purpose is to experience and enjoy something and then record it. The children are used to recording experiences in a variety of different ways and using words is a natural extension of this. The experience is real and stays with them, which gives an immediacy to their writing:

> Children who struggle with the mechanics and composition of a story can get a vision in their head and think of words to convey it. In Y1 [ages 5–6] I might begin to draft with them but not in Reception. It gives them the confidence to try, write and achieve.

With very young children Lorna will just allow them to choose and arrange their own words. As they gain in confidence she will suggest ways of improving their writing and work with them both individually and in small groups on this. This might mean a change of order, it might mean adding an alliterative adjective or it might mean finding a more powerful word. Whatever happens, Lorna is careful to keep ownership of the writing strictly with the child. The ultimate decision is the child's and if the child is happy with the poem that is a sign of success. The child's ability to make such a judgement comes from the huge amount and variety of poetry that has been heard and responded to.

Conclusions: Where do I Start in Teaching Poetry?

Lorna is often asked by other teachers for some ideas about how to teach poetry and she told me how difficult she finds it to answer this question. It is not about knowing a few teaching strategies and applying them to a few key poems. Lorna admits that her love for sharing poetry with her children comes from her passion for poetry itself. Lorna loves poetry as a reader for its own sake and the power of her teaching is that she is sharing what she loves with fellow readers. The fact that these fellow readers are aged 5 is almost irrelevant. Lorna wants them to enjoy the poems she enjoys as much as she does.

In their report on the teaching of poetry, Ofsted (2007) said:

> Many teachers, especially in the primary schools, did not know enough about poetry. This sometimes led to poor quality marking and a uniformity in practice, where the same few poems were studied across most schools. Although these poems were mostly worth studying, many of them were relatively lightweight and pupils had only limited experience of classic poems and poems from other cultures and traditions. Weaknesses in subject knowledge also reduced the quality of teachers' feedback to pupils on the poetry they had written. (p. 4)

It could not be said that the poems enjoyed by the children in Lorna's class were lightweight and neither was the children's experience limited, but this was because of Lorna's own personal experience as a reader of poetry herself. She had experienced the emotion and imagination of the poet and shared that with her class. Other teachers of young children to whom I have spoken recognise the importance of their own subject knowledge when it comes to teaching poetry. A Reception class teacher in a different setting talked to me about how she struggles with teaching poetry:

> I can't understand it myself and I think it's difficult to teach something you don't understand yourself. I can never work out what poetry means – it's difficult, isn't it? I think poetry is really hard. I work on nursery rhymes a lot but not poetry really. At this age it's just about rhyme really, isn't it.

Lorna has the confidence and knowledge to understand what poetry can do and she knows the poems well enough to allow them to work in the reader's mind and imagination. That is the key to effective teaching of poetry with young children. In Lorna's words:

> They ask me how do you teach poetry – you don't. You read them. You give them a high profile. You explore them with children – they will make what they will of it. You expose them to rich language and let them play with it.

SOMETHING TO THINK ABOUT

When was the last time you read and enjoyed poetry at your own level? Explore poetry anthologies, written for children or adults, and think about how they make you want to respond. Get to know one or two really well.

SOMETHING TO READ

Spend time exploring the children's poetry archive (www.poetryarchive.org/childrensarchive) and get to know one or two poets well.

SOMETHING TO DO

Read a poem a day to your class – any poem will do. Just read it several times, encourage the children to join in, have the text somewhere for them to read independently and enjoy it together.

References

Brice Heath, S. (1983) *Ways with Words: Language, Life and Work in Communities and Classrooms*. Cambridge: Cambridge University Press.

Bruce, T. & Spratt, J. (2008) *Essentials of Literacy from 0–7: Children's Journeys into Literacy*. London: SAGE.

Bryant, P. & Bradley, L. (1985) *Children's Reading Problems*. Oxford: Blackwell.

Bryant, P. & Goswami, U. (1987) 'Phonological Awareness and Learning to Read', in J.R. Beech & A.M. Colley (eds) *Cognitive Approaches to Reading*. Chichester: Wiley.

Carroll, L. (1872) 'Jabberwocky', in *Through the Looking-Glass and What Alice Found There*. London: Macmillan.

Causley, C. (1970) *Figgie Hobbin: Poems for Children*. London: Macmillan.

Cremin, T., Mottram, M., Collins, F., Powell, S. & Safford, K. (2009) 'Teachers as Readers: Building Communities of Readers', *Literacy*, 43(1): 11–19.

Cummings, E.E. (1994) 'maggie and millie and mollie and may', in *The Complete Poems: 1904–1962*, ed. G.J. Firmage. New York: Norton.

Department for Children, Schools and Families (DCSF) (2008) *Progression in Poetry*. Available at http://nationalstrategies.standards.dcsf.gov.uk/node/98404?uc=force-uj

Department for Children, Schools and Families (DCSF) (2008) *Statutory Framework for the Early Years Foundation Stage*. London: DCSF.

Department for Education and Skills (DfES) (2006) *Primary Framework for Literacy and Mathematics*. London: DfES.

Dillon, L. & Dillon, D. (2002) *Rap a Tap Tap: Here's Bojangles – Think of That*. New York: The Blue Sky Press.

Edgar, M. (1978) *The Lion and Albert*. London: Methuen.

Kipling. R. (1906) 'A Smuggler's Song' in *Puck of Pook's Hill*. London: Macmillan.

Lear, E. (1871) 'The Owl and the Pussy Cat', in *Nonsense Songs and Stories*. London: Warne.

Lear, E. (1947) 'The Pobble Who Had No Toes', in *The Complete Nonsense of Edward Lear*. London: Faber & Faber.

Milligan, S. (1997) 'On the Ning Nang Nong', in *Complete Poems*. London: Penguin.

Noyes, A. (1999) *The Highwayman*, illus. C. Keeping. Oxford: Oxford University Press.

Ofsted (2007) *Poetry in Schools: A Survey of Practice 2006–7*. London: Ofsted.

Richards, L. (1902) 'Eletelephony', available at: http://oldpoetry.com/opoem/41631-Laura-Elizabeth-Richards-Eletelephony-wbr-

Stevenson, R.L. (1885) 'From a Railway Carriage', available at: http://oldpoetry.com/opoem/show/7657-Robert-Louis-Stevenson-From-A-Railway-Carriage

Thomas, D. (1961) 'Poetic Manifesto', *Texas Quarterly*, 4(4) (Winter): 44–53.

Webb, S. (2003) *Tanka Tanka Skunk*. London: Red Fox.

Whitehead, M. (2010) *Language and Literacy in the Early Years 0–7*, 4th edn. London: SAGE.

Wordsworth, W. (1815) 'Daffodils', available at: http://oldpoetry.com/opoem/2902-William-Wordsworth--I-wandered-lonely-as-a-cloud

Chapter 3

Actual Poems,
Possible Responses

Prue Goodwin

CHAPTER OVERVIEW

This chapter describes the author's approach to teaching poetry in the junior school (7–11 years). 'Actual Poems, Possible Responses' – a title deliberately copied from Jerome Bruner's work (1986) – reflects on what often actually happens when children read poetry in primary schools and what is possible. Seeing the role of teachers as central to success, the chapter concentrates on how they engage children with poetry by focusing on children's response to poetry, encouraging thoughtful discussion about a range of poems, and engaging children's imaginative capabilities to express their understanding. Suggestions are offered as to how teachers can prepare both themselves and their classes to study poetry, along with titles of useful books and examples of practical approaches.

A Passion for Poetry

'What does glitter-drizzle sound like?'

The 10-year-old girl who asked this question was surrounded by the rest of her class, working in small groups and experimenting with a range of musical instruments. She continued: 'And we're not sure which instrument to use for "almost breaths of air". Can we just use our mouths?' The room was noisy but everyone was totally absorbed in the task of finding a way to represent with musical sound the vocabulary used by Seamus Heaney in his poem 'Rain Stick' from the collection *Spirit Level* (1996). The children had about 20 minutes to prepare and rehearse their work. Eventually, it was time to perform. Silence fell. Each group of children had used a watery phrase from the poem – 'down-pour, sluice-rush, spillage', 'like a gutter stopping tickling' and 'sprinkle of drops' – to inspire an improvised phrase of music. As the poem was read aloud, each theme was played – rising to a crescendo then fading as the next phrase came in. At the final line 'Listen now again' everyone played again and gradually came to a stop. Silence. A magical silence until we whooped with delight and pride.

Robert handed me his writing, a cheeky grin across his face. He watched me as I read his work:

Poems

Oh NO! Not poems!

What shall I put?

What about school?

No.

What about homework?

No.

What about art?

Might be okay, but no.

What about French?

Not much to write about there.

What about maths?

Too boring.

What about creative writing?

Too boring still.

What about teachers?

Far too boring, so no.

Ah! I know, I'll write about poems.

by Robert

After two terms in Year 6, Robert was actually producing some work. He was what is known as a 'statemented' child – not for any lack of ability, but because he simply refused to put pen to paper. A work-refuser. Of course, when he handed me the poem, he was intelligent enough to know he was relinquishing some power by actually enjoying an English lesson and, as a boy with a keen sense of humour, he also knew how ironic it was to be writing about what he would normally refuse to do. The 'by Robert' at the end was a defiant assertion. His favourite words, *boring* and *no*, featured throughout his work and he managed to express negative thoughts about every aspect of school – except one. In the last line of his writing, Robert implicitly acknowledges that poetry is not boring, in fact it inspires him to write. Reading Robert's work and listening to the 'symphony' created to accompany 'Rain Stick' were two of the most rewarding moments of my long teaching career.

When I started teaching in a primary school there was no National Curriculum, no Literacy Strategy nor any other government initiative to tell me how to teach. Nor were there Ofsted inspectors to check that I was doing as I was told. However, during my first year as a teacher, it never occurred to me not to share poetry with the children in my care. When I was a child, listening to and reading poetry had always given me pleasure; now that I was teaching, surely every child was entitled to the same pleasurable literary experiences that I had had at school. By the time I was teaching Robert, I had been teaching for more than a decade and had increased my professional qualifications considerably. I had an academic understanding of the importance of studying poetry with youngsters. As a result, I could see how all their learning had benefited; the experience of poetry had helped my pupils to understand complex ideas, to consider unfamiliar things more closely and to find ways to express their thinking more clearly.

Recent government initiatives in the UK on teaching literacy have been interpreted, possibly mistakenly, in ways that make it possible to assume that the purpose of teaching poetry is solely as an intellectual exercise. Educational publishers produced ready-made lessons through which to instruct pupils in the use of figurative language (simile, metaphor, alliteration, etc.), different poetic forms (sonnet, haiku, rap, etc.) and knowledge of a prescribed list of 'classic' English verse. All these different elements of poetic writing have their place and should be present in the curriculum, but taught in isolation from personal response, none is likely to promote a love of poetry if approached in a didactic way. To value poetry it must speak to a reader, catch the attention and awaken an expectation of enjoyment. Children need to be excited by the language, content and unpredictability of poetry and to be encouraged to express confidently their personal responses to the work of poets to whom they are introduced, knowing that their opinions will be valued.

This chapter is about working with primary pupils to achieve a love of poetry as well as some understanding of how it works. Sharing poetry is at the heart of the chapter – reading it, writing it, talking about it, responding to it – not as part of some required list of educational tasks but because it provides pleasure, extends thinking and offers linguistic empowerment. Ensuring that all children in their care have positive experiences with poetry should be the first concern of teachers. Once engaged with poetry, children need to:

- be read to
- be given opportunities to read widely themselves
- respond in a variety of ways to what they have read
- be supported in finding their own poetic voices as independent writers.

The rest of this chapter sets out to support primary practitioners in achieving all these aims.

Poetry is Personal

Competent teachers ensure that they have sufficient knowledge and under-standing of what they teach. The most effective teachers, however, go beyond a functional level of information or skill in order to communicate an enthusiasm for a subject. Teachers who demonstrate a love of it themselves are more likely to infect their pupils with a delight in reading, writing and responding to poetry. Enjoyment is an emotional response and thus very personal. Every teacher will develop their own preferences and, although there will be plenty of advice from a variety of sources (including this book), it is important that teachers realise that someone else's favourite poems will not necessarily be theirs. We all need to prepare to teach poetry by reading widely in order to gather our own selection of poems, as there is no doubt we teach best the literature that we love. Learning to love poetry may be the first step in preparing to teach it.

When I started my career I had a tremendous advantage over some of my colleagues because, not only had I loved poetry from a very early age, but nothing during my own schooling had put me off it. As a result, I had a store of favourites that were easy to incorporate into my teaching; it seemed natural to do so and it gave me and, I hope, my pupils great pleasure. Although I was lucky to have had a positive childhood experience, it was not essential. An appreciation of poetry can be developed at any time and many colleagues have discovered and learned to love poetry without anybody's help. Most often, however, acquiring an appreciation of poetry has come through being taught by inspiring educators, enthusiasts who have shared their passion with their pupils.

Not everyone who becomes a primary teacher has a love of poetry but all are required to teach it as part of the curriculum for English, just as we are expected to teach magnetism in science or multiplication in maths. A recent survey of over a thousand primary teachers revealed that many colleagues had very lim-ited knowledge of children's poets (Cremin et al., 2008) and, whilst I have no verifiable evidence of this fact, several teachers have confessed to not knowing 'what to do with a poem' when attending literature courses. Before anyone attempts to teach poetry, it is critical that feelings of negativity or inadequacy are acknowledged and dealt with or those attitudes may inadvertently get handed on to the next generation.

I firmly believe that everyone can find poetry that they like if they are willing to look and that 'all teachers who read poems can teach poetry, and all teachers can use all kinds of poems to teach with, including adult poems' (Hull, 2010: 1). So for those colleagues who feel insecure about the whole enterprise, there follows some suggestions which could help you to find a selection of poems that you would want to share with your class.

Reading for Yourself: Preparing to Teach

Here are some tips about reading for your own enjoyment:

- Always browse through a book, stopping to read more deeply when a poem takes your fancy. You don't have to read every poem in the book.
- You don't have to like a poem because someone says you should. You can take it or leave it. Good poets write poor poetry sometimes and not everything will be to your taste.
- Give each poem you choose a chance. Take your time. Spend as long as you wish on any book or preferred poet. Re-read things that you like. The more you read a poem the more you will find in it.
- Read a poem so that it makes sense – follow the meanings of the words. Don't worry too much about line-endings even when they rhyme. A good poet will have taken care of the syntax as well as the rhythm of the words.
- Read a lot of different sorts of poetry by a variety of poets. There is huge diversity in content, mood and form of poetry: obscure and simple; profound and flippant; humorous and serious; sentimental and severe; comforting and disturbing; and, treasure and trash. If you find any poem boring, embarrassing, confusing or excluding – move on to a different one.

Responding to Poetry

Response is reaction to an experience or stimulus. Readers always respond in some way to what they read. An initial response is usually a feeling – amusement, boredom, excitement or irritation – that may be unexpressed at the time but which becomes conscious thought when formed into a spoken opinion. Articulating thoughts about what has been read helps to clarify and explain initial feelings, whilst discussion with others refines response by clarifying it further or causing us to reconsider it. Positive reactions to a text may inspire us to present our response in a different form; for example, through imaginative activities, such as writing or other creative arts. Feeling, thinking, talking and, occasionally, taking action are all aspects of response which teachers may call on to encourage children to become engaged in a poem. Response may involve:

- expressing feelings – how does it make you feel?
- articulating thoughts – what does it make you think?
- discussing ideas – engagement in authentic dialogue
- discussing the language – how do the words work?
- using imagination – does it inspire your imagination?
- production and performance – can you represent your feelings, thoughts, imagination through a creative activity?

It is completely unrealistic (and unnecessary) to respond in all these ways every time a poem is read. Sometimes you must read poetry aloud to your class for the sheer pleasure of listening to it. When that happens, there is no need for children to say or do anything. I would usually ask, 'Did you like that?' but while some children clamour to tell you, others are entitled not to put their feelings into words. On other occasions you may encourage them to chat quietly with each other or to compare notes on which poems they enjoyed most (you can ensure that copies are available for them to read when they wish). When there is a more specific learning intention, focused discussion drawing on and validating children's opinions is fundamental to the process. The involvement of creative activity in response to a poem engages children's imaginations and offers a means other than linguistic with which to express their response.

Talking: Sharing Feelings, Thoughts and Ideas

The majority of effective classroom practices used for teaching literacy are either directly to do with, or have their roots in, dialogue. As Robin Alexander points out in the report of the Cambridge Primary Review: 'Language, and especially spoken language, is identified in the research on children's cognitive development as one of the keys to thinking, understanding and learning from the earliest age and throughout the primary phase' (2010: 305). Alexander established this argument in the book *Towards Dialogic Teaching* (3rd edn, 2006) where he identifies clearly the benefits of children engaging in authentic conversations with their teachers and with each other. Such conversations in the context of learning are not arbitrary but based on the principles that underpin 'dialogic teaching'.

Dialogic teaching is:

- *collective*: teachers and children address learning tasks together, whether as a group or as a class, rather than in isolation
- *reciprocal*: teachers and children listen to each other, share ideas and consider alternative viewpoints

- *supportive*: children articulate their ideas freely, without fear of embarrassment over 'wrong' answers; and they help each other to reach common understandings
- *cumulative*: teachers and children build on their own and each others' ideas and chain them into coherent lines of thinking and enquiry
- *purposeful*: teachers plan and steer classroom talk with particular educational goals in view. (Alexander, 2006: 38)

Alexander continues his description in similar academic style, yet close examination of his words reveals that the formal and functional sounding 'purposeful dialogue' should include children (and teachers) being encouraged to take time to think, listen carefully, share and respect viewpoints, and to address questions in depth rather than worry about giving a 'correct' answer. These statements resonate with the work of Aidan Chambers on booktalk which he explains in *Tell Me: Children, Reading and Talk* (1993):

> As an activity 'Tell me' booktalk is individual and at the same time communal and cooperative, for each participant must listen to what others have to say and take account of what everyone else thinks the text is about. (p. 21)

A supportive way to engage children in discussion about a poem is for them to take part in a booktalk session. Chambers suggests that, as a means of getting a conversation going, children share the 'enthusiasms, puzzles (i.e. difficulties) and connections (i.e. patterns)' that they find in a text. This 'three way' guidance into discussion works as well for a poem as it does for a book because 'booktalk is a way of giving form to the thoughts and emotions stimulated by a [poem] and by the meaning(s) we make together' (Chambers, 1993: 20). Genuine dialogue about poetry between children and their teachers leads to the truth-seeking, open-minded thinking necessary to enable youngsters to understand meanings and appreciate the crafting of a poet's words:

> Far better that the children explore a poem, respond to the bits that interest them, and slowly piece together the parts into a coherent whole. Poems need to be experienced rather than explained. The main emphasis of the teacher's job is not, in fact, *explication du texte* but the cultivation of individual and shared responses to the text. (Benton & Fox, 1990: 24)

There is no failsafe formula for engaging children with poetry and eliciting their response. Teachers will discover ways that work best for them with their classes. The rest of this chapter offers practical suggestions for encouraging response to poetry. The suggestions are based on poems and approaches that I used throughout my career in primary schools. I offer them in the spirit of sharing but be warned: purists may strongly disapprove of the methods I adopt in order to achieve my aims when teaching. For example, I often break lines and phrases up or divide the poem into short chunks, but – trust me – my intention is always to motivate in children a desire to 'own' the poem for themselves. Whatever else may happen, work always begins with engagement with the whole poem and delight in the poet's voice.

Performing Poems

Reading aloud is the best way to introduce poetry to children. Each 'read aloud' is a performance, so always rehearse it, remembering to read naturally but with a little bit of drama to liven it up for your audience. Your reading is a model of how to read a poem – whether aloud or in your head. When I first meet a class, I usually read aloud a collection of poems which demonstrate the diversity of poetry, for example:

- an extract from 'Pen Rhythm' by Benjamin Zephaniah in *Ink-slinger* (Styles & Cook, 1990)
- 'Some rhymes are a sight and some are really sound' by Brian Patten (1992) in *Thawing Frozen Frogs*
- 'The Thought-Fox' by Ted Hughes in *Ink-slinger*
- 'Forbidden poem' by Tony Mitton (1998) in *Plum*
- 'The Robin' by June Crebbin (2005) in *The Crocodile is Coming!*

Once children have enough experience of listening to adults reading aloud, most will be very happy to read their poetry choices aloud too. Sharing poetry in this way is a valuable use of time and should be a regular part of primary school life.

If you intend the children to study the poem in depth, it is important that they hear the poem read aloud several times. I often use an approach which gradually gets them all joining in, and for which I have prepared the poem in advance. The process follows this pattern:

1. I read the poem while the children listen.
2. Children are given a copy of the poem to follow as I read it again. (They can now see how the lines work – how they look on the page and how they sound when read aloud.)
3. For a third reading the children are invited to read along with me. (About three-quarters of the class usually do.)
4. I ask all children to read along for a fourth 'performance'. (Even if they don't join in, all are following the copy and become more familiar with the way each line functions as part of a whole.)
5. I then ask, 'Who would like to read it aloud without me?' (Hands go up.) 'You could do it with a friend or two.' (More hands go up.)
6. 'Oh dear, too many to do individual readings. Let's do a shared read aloud. Choose a friend (or two) to read with. ' (The poem has been prepared by

being divided into short sections and numbered in order. I give out sections, differentiating by difficulty of text so the less confident readers can easily manage their lines. Children have a few minutes to practise before they read. They arrange themselves, standing in the order of the poem, and have a run-through before the final performance.)

7. 'One, two, three ...!' (I 'conduct' and support those readers who stumble and we keep reading to the end. Applause! We are applauding ourselves. There is no audience and yet the atmosphere of 'performance' is electric. There is a sense of corporate achievement in the joint enterprise. It is now *our* poem.)

Although children need time to get used to this approach, I have found that it works every time – even with longer poems such as T.S. Eliot's 'Macavity – The Mystery Cat' and Alfred Noyes' 'The Highwayman'.

Exploring a Poem

Thinking deeply, looking closely and responding creatively increase interest in a poem as well as enabling readers to find deeper meanings. Returning to a text to clarify meaning always enhances understanding. The purpose of exploring a poem is to become intimate with it, get to know the content, feel comfortable with the language, gain insight to the deeper meanings and recognise the significance of the vocabulary choices. It helps if children have a task that involves using their creative skills; drawing and drama are especially useful in focusing their thoughts on a poem.

'The Listeners', 'Macavity' and 'The Highwayman' (all of which can be found in Kaye Webb's (1979) anthology *I Like this Poem*), are good examples of poems that lend themselves to some guided 'exploration' and imaginative response. They are a little too sophisticated for primary pupils to fully understand without some 'scaffolding' supplied by an adult, as illustrated below, yet have the potential to really delight youngsters:

- Following a shared read aloud of 'Macavity' (from *Old Possum's Book of Practical Cats*), and a discussion, the children were given a 'Police Department File' to record Macavity's criminal activities. It included space to put a recent picture, physical description, paw print and a Confidential Report on the list of his suspected crimes. Wanted posters came next, followed by an improvised trial scene.
- Reading and discussing 'The Highwayman' was followed by retelling through dramatic improvisation. The re-enactment featured a cast of very suspicious characters and enthusiastically produced sound effects (get out the coconut shells!). Using the picturebook version of the poem, illustrated by Charles Keeping, considerably enhanced our enjoyment of this classic tale.

● 'The Listeners' is spooky; remember this when reading aloud and get the children to retell the story in a darkened room. To illustrate the poem, it is fun to make an old ruin out of a box. Windows and doors cut out in the walls of the 'ruin' can be used to look through, into the inside of the box where the phantoms can be depicted standing on the staircase. Children can make an individual haunted ruin by using paper-folding techniques (see Paul Johnson's (2000) *Making Books* for basic and advanced ideas about using paper technology to support literacy development).

Exploring the Language of Poetry

Exploring the way words function in a poem can be enjoyable. The opening discussion about a poem asks questions such as 'How does it make you feel? What does it make you think?' Looking at the language helps to answer the next question, 'How does the poet use words to make us feel and think that way?' However, beware of the trap of linguistic analysis. Searching for metaphors or alliteration as a separate activity from the effect and meaning of a poem leads to the sort of lessons that have put people off poetry for life. Asking pupils to spot and name metaphors, similes and other elements of figurative language is pointless unless it is within the context of personal response. When children have enjoyed a poem, there must be a purpose for seeking out particular words. For example, if the children are going to respond through art or music to 'The Highwayman' they need to investigate the poem to find the visual descriptions or to discover where sound effects would be appropriate.

If the purpose of your lesson is to introduce poetic devices and terminology, at least do it with verses that the children can understand with ease. For example, June Crebbin writes brilliantly for children; she incorporates figurative language in ways that they can appreciate. For instance, look at the simple and effective use of simile in 'My Rabbit':

> When my rabbit
> is out in his run,
>
> he digs up the ground
> like a dog,
>
> washes himself
> like a squirrel,
>
> sits on his back legs
> like a kangaroo,

leaps and twirls
like an acrobat

and

when he eats a cabbage leaf,
as is his daily habit,
he delicately nibbles it
EXACTLY like a rabbit!

And the unobtrusive thread of the textile metaphor in 'The Cobweb Morning':

On Monday morning
We do spellings and maths.
And silent reading.

But on the Monday
After the frost
We went straight outside.

Cobwebs hung in the cold air,
Everywhere.
All around the playground,
They clothed the trees,
Dressed every bush
In veils of fine white lace.

Each web,
A wheel of patient spinning.
Each spider,
Hidden,
Waiting.

Inside,
We worked all morning
To capture the outside.

Now
In our patterns and poems
We remember
The cobweb morning.

These beautifully crafted poems, with their reflection on childhood experience, invite young readers in. They can enjoy the poems at the same time as considering vocabulary choices, so do not have to untangle unfamiliar meanings or tackle new vocabulary whilst learning about figurative language. Even with older primary pupils, an easily accessible writing style assists their understanding of literary language. June Crebbin is one of many contemporary poets who write poems that children love without shying away from the literary conventions. Brian Patten, Allan Ahlberg, Jackie Kay, Tony Mitton, Valerie Bloom, Michael Rosen and Benjamin Zephaniah are among many others who never condescend to children by writing down to them. There is no need to look further than a good children's poetry anthology to find simple examples of poetic language used by expert wordsmiths.

Conclusion

Let's return to the beginning of this chapter with children preparing their musical response to Seamus Heaney's poem 'Rain Stick'. The class had discussed feelings, thoughts, ideas, language – especially how the words had suggested ideas about music and water – and had collaborated in the creation of a musical composition.

A rain stick is a hollow tube, usually a dried out cactus stalk, with seeds or grit trapped inside. The sound of the seeds running from end to end of the hollow cactus stalk provides the comforting swash and swish sound of water. Originally it was used as an instrument of magic, possibly in the hands of a tribal shaman in Central America as he invoked the 'gods' to provide life-giving rain. Heaney's poem encapsulates the possible literal, metaphorical and spiritual interpretations which can be inspired by the sound of a rain stick. The poem is a challenging text to use with primary pupils, but well within the grasp of a class of 10- and 11-year-olds if presented to them in ways that reveal the different levels of meaning in the poem.

So often, the way in which poetry is presented in primary schools can be as uninspiring as seeds rattling through a dried up stick. But a rain stick is an instrument of magic when in the hands of the shaman. It takes the power of the shaman to make the rain stick effective, to invoke the gods to bring life to the parched earth. No matter how many poets write for children, how many books about teaching poetry are available, or what curriculum documents demand, it takes the commitment, care and creativity of good teachers to bring poetry alive for primary pupils. And when they do, the magic works, and experiencing all the pleasures of poetry is made possible for children.

SOMETHING TO THINK ABOUT

Developing children's response to poetry requires teachers to be innovative and creative themselves. Teachers need to model all forms of imaginative response for their pupils as well as being able to support children with drama, music and dance and to express ideas through art and design. Your own creative strengths may lie in aspects of problem solving or invention. These aspects of creative thinking can also be harnessed in response to literature. Are you able to draw on your own creative resources in order to engage your pupils in imaginative response? Remember, when responding to any literature, it is the process of being creative not the end product that matters.

SOMETHING TO READ

There are some poetry books that I will always use when teaching. Several have already been mentioned in this chapter. Here are a few more titles that I regularly enjoy:

- Allan Ahlberg, *Friendly Matches* (2001)
- Carol Ann Duffy, *The Good Child's Guide to Rock and Roll* (2003)
- Jackie Kay, *Two's Company* (1992)
- Kenneth Koch & Kate Farrell, *Talking to the Sun* (1986)
- Jonarno Lawson, *Inside Out* (2008)
- Grace Nichols, *Paint Me a Poem* (2004)

There are many more, but by far the best thing would be for you to build your own collection. Once you take that personal step to put your own delight in poetry at the heart of your teaching, you will have a store of reading for life.

SOMETHING TO DO

Begin your search for personal preference by reading poetry written specifically for children. *The Puffin Book of Utterly Brilliant Poetry*, edited by Brian Patten (1998), would be a good starting point as it has writing from an excellent selection of contemporary children's writers.

Then look through an anthology which presents a broad range of verse suitable to share with children; for example, *I Like This Poem* (edited by Kaye Webb, 1979) or *Because a Fire was in my Head* (edited by Michael Morpurgo, 2001).

Next, browse through a good general anthology, such as *The Rattle Bag* (edited by Seamus Heaney & Ted Hughes, 1982), to get a sense of just how much there is to choose from.

When you feel confident, select a small collection of poems that you feel will appeal and read them aloud to your class. Do it purely for the pleasure of listening to the poems. Make no demands on the listeners other than asking whether they liked them or not. Don't follow up with any 'work' beyond possibly asking them to decide on their favourites.

Before transferring your personal exploration of poetry into plans for your classroom, read *Love that Dog* by Sharon Creech (2002). Although a long way from being a textbook or set of instructions, it provides a model for teaching poetry and a sense of how rewarding it can be to introduce children to the words of great poets whilst also helping youngsters to find their own poetic voices.

References

Alexander, R. (2006) *Towards Dialogic Teaching*. York: Dialogos.

Alexander, R. (2010) *Children, their World, their Education*. Abingdon: Routledge.

Ahlberg, A. (2001) *Friendly Matches*. London: Viking.

Benton, M. & Fox, G. (1990) *Teaching Literature: Nine to Fourteen*. Oxford: Oxford University Press.

Bruner, J.S. (1986) *Actual Minds, Possible Worlds*. Cambridge, MA: Harvard University Press.

Chambers, A. (1993) *Tell me: Children, Reading and Talk*. Stroud: Thimble Press.

Crebbin, J. (2005) *The Crocodile is Coming!* London: Walker Books.

Creech, S. (2002) *Love That Dog*. London: Bloomsbury.

Cremin, T., Bearne, E., Mottram, M. and Goodwin, P. (2008) 'Exploring teachers' knowledge of children's literature', *The Cambridge Journal of Education*, 38(4): 449–64.

Duffy, C.A. (2003) *The Good Child's Guide to Rock and Roll*. London: Faber & Faber.

Heaney, S. (1996) *Spirit Level*. London: Faber & Faber.

Heaney, S. & Hughes, T. (eds) (1982) *The Rattle Bag*. London: Faber & Faber.

Hull, R. (2010) *Poetry: From Reading to Writing*. London: David Fulton.

Johnson, P. (2000) *Making Books*. London: A&C Black.

Kay, J. (1992) *Two's Company*. London: Blackie Children's Books.

Koch, K. & Farrell, K. (1986) *Talking to the Sun*. London: Viking.

Lawson, J. (2008) *Inside Out*. London: Walker.

Mitton, T. (1998) *Plum*. London: Scholastic.

Morpurgo, M. (ed.) (2001) *Because a Fire was in my Head*. London: Faber & Faber.

Nichols, G. (2004) *Paint Me a Poem: New Poems Inspired by Art in the Tate*. London: A&C Black.

Noyes, A. (1999) *The Highwayman*. Oxford: Oxford University Press.

Patten, B. (ed.) (1998) *The Puffin Book of Utterly Brilliant Poetry*. London: Penguin.

Patten, B. (1992) *Thawing Frozen Frogs*. London: Puffin.

Styles, M. & Cook, H. (1990) *Ink-slinger*. London: A&C Black.

Webb, K. (1979) *I Like This Poem*. London: Puffin.

Chapter 4

Making Poetry

Catriona Nicholson

CHAPTER OVERVIEW

The chapter proposes that through early encounters and sympathetic teaching the celebration of poetry can be engaged with as a lasting literary experience. It draws significantly on the approaches to poetry writing in the classroom documented by Jill Pirrie and Ted Hughes and also on related reflections of a range of contemporary poets. Quoting extensively from children's writing, the chapter argues that, given the guidance and encouragement to closely observe the human and physical world around them, and the freedom to explore their creative impulses, children can express their ideas in accomplished poetic forms. As a framework for these examples, reference is made to the writer's own teaching approaches and strategies.

You have to inhabit poetry

If you want to make it.

(from 'Making Poetry', Stevenson, 2005: 17)

The poet Anne Stevenson writes of a childhood spent in the company of parents whose love of poetry and music became a wellspring of inspiration for her own creativity. She refers to this formative time as growing up in 'the house of poetry' (Stevenson and O'Siadhail, 1989: 6).

In his Introduction to this book, Michael Lockwood writes of how an English teacher's positive valuing of 'creativity and imagination' in his pupils and the way poetry was brought alive for that 1960s class, has left a lifelong legacy of delight in at least one pupil: Michael describes how he himself has inherited his teacher's love of literature and thereby has passed on that enthusiasm to other generations of teachers and pupils. His experience of having been finely taught and, in turn, handing down the energy and richness of that teaching, is an affirming advocacy for the credo 'pass it on boys, pass it on' delivered to impressionable pupils by the maverick English teacher, Douglas Hector, in Alan Bennett's play *The History Boys* (2004).

As teachers we pass on the best of our own learning, teaching best what we know and love best, and hoping always that children will be influenced by our enthusiasms. As English teachers we are purveyors of words and meanings, and in order for us to bring poetry alive, to help children 'make' poetry, we must, as Anne Stevenson suggests, 'inhabit' the art and craft of it, the song and the dance of it.

The headteacher of the Somerset junior school where I took up my first post in the 1960s was someone who put poetry at the heart of the curriculum. His quietly conveyed Quaker convictions nurtured his teaching philosophy and I was taken on because (as he disclosed after the interview) he quickly saw that literature mattered to me. I recall that much of the interview was a lively discussion about his and my interest in the poet Edward Thomas. Framed and writ large on the staffroom wall was a single text, four lines from a poem by Robert Bridges:

> I love all beauteous things;
>
> I seek and adore them …
>
> … I too will something make
>
> And joy in the making! (Bridges, 1953: 281)

These lines acted as the school's mission statement and decades on, still teaching poetry, I remain faithful to the conviction and guiding influence of my first wise Head. He exemplified for my colleagues and me how delight and learning come through 'making'. The 'making of poetry' referred to by Stevenson, the 'inhabiting', the 'inheriting', have shaped and enriched my lines of thought and belief for decades.

The Influence of Jill Pirrie

Much has been written about the teaching of poetry writing in primary schools but I have always found myself drawn to the work and passionate commitment of Jill Pirrie whose beliefs and ideals in terms of English teaching matched my own. In her book *On Common Ground: A Programme for Teaching Poetry* (1988), Jill Pirrie outlined her role as a facilitator for the creative accomplishments of her pupils, testifying to the centrality of literature as a reference and an inspiration for her teaching.

A few years later she discussed her ideas in more detail in an article 'Giants, Castles and Moonlit Apples' (Pirrie, 1992), explaining how her love of literary forms and her search for self-knowledge has provided her with a framework of reference for working alongside children in the classroom. In this article she developed her ideas about the power and impact of literature and described how this formative force influenced her thinking and led her to teach poetry in a Suffolk middle school, believing that once children are able to 'assimilate the forms and symbols of their literary culture they achieve the mastery of language which will set them free' (p. 5). The kinship she sees between literature and literacy is manifestly exemplified when she writes about writing, the process and the product. Drawing on Richard Church's account in *Over the Bridge* (1955) of his development as a poet, she describes how she became aware that the formative, creative, process he documents can find its essential parallels in the growth of 'each one of us as a human being' (Pirrie, 1992: 5). In the Introduction to her second book on the teaching of poetry *Apple Fire* (1993) she reiterated her belief that the power of poetry is the basis of language work. She sees language in terms defined by the Newbolt report as 'the element in which we live and work' (Newbolt, 1921: 20) – not so much a repertoire of skills to be learned but 'one of the forms of being' (Knight, 1994: v). In elaborating on this she submitted that poetry, myth, fable, story are 'forms and symbols of the language' and through familiarity with and an understanding of these forms 'children come to know themselves and the grammar within which they will make meaning' (Pirrie, 1993: 19). Taking a mild swipe at restrictive practices that have tended to straitjacket the English curriculum over the past few decades, Pirrie believes that children respond intuitively and creatively to wisely mediated experiences of poetry:

> Certainly, poetry can be the most effective basis for our teaching of English. As the most highly disciplined form of writing, it makes the greatest demands and is a sure path to literacy. It is not enough to put children through certain grammatical hoops on the false assumption that they will emerge literate and competent … Instead we must return to the richness of our culture and immerse them in its literary forms and then help them to find their own voice within that culture. (1988: 85)

Pirrie's closest mentor has been Ted Hughes and, like many of us who have turned to his poetry and writing for reassurance and delight, she has been sustained, during bleak and alienating periods of educational flux and change, by his advice to teachers which, she contends, 'assert[s] a proper priority' and 'transcend[s] the vagaries of fashion' (1992: 5). She reminds us of what Hughes declares in *Poetry in the Making*: '[Teachers'] words should be not "How to write" but "How to say what you really mean" – which is part of the search for self-knowledge and perhaps in one form or another, grace' (Hughes, 1986: 12). Pirrie's gift as a teacher has been to instill in her pupils a sense of 'strength, courage and intelligence', encouraging them to 'say what they really mean' and in doing so taking them on what she has called 'a rigorous route to literacy' (Pirrie, 1993: 16).

Referring to the process of writing poetry, she believes that children need to become totally involved in the act of thinking, looking, listening. Such involvement is a form of imaginative reflection during which they, as poets, reveal 'the surprising within the ordinary' (Pirrie, 1988: 17). Thus the apparently unremarkable, everyday experience can be transformed into a source of excitement or special interest: the young writer recognises that his or her own experience attains new value by being articulated and 'revealed' in a new way. The good English teacher, therefore, 'must provide new perspectives on the ordinary world' (Pirrie, 1993: 15).

Pirrie describes how experiences of literature can generate creativity in young writers. Her belief is that such fertile moments, in terms of response to literature, are prompted by feelings of connection with a text, 'when we recognize something we have noticed ourselves but never before truly realized, something that has been brought to our attention by the seeing eye of the writer' (1988: 1).

Seamus Heaney believes that 'poems and rhymes, especially if they are known by heart, appeal to memory and open a path towards further meaning' (Heaney, 2004: 4). Like Anne Stevenson and Jill Pirrie, I was fortunate to grow up in 'a house of poetry' and that early enriching mulch of memorised word-sound and song, widened and deepened at school through the guidance of inspirational English teachers, has provided a sure foundation for personal delight and, throughout my teaching career, for working with young writers. As an English teacher I have wanted to explore and maybe 'extend [the] franchise' (Wilson, 2001: 4) entrusted to teachers like Jill Pirrie by Ted Hughes. Sharpening a child's perception of the physical and human world around them and transforming, bringing radiance to the seemingly mundane, has been central to my teaching in primary schools. I have wanted children, and students training to be teachers, to absorb some of the literature that has delighted me; to learn to 'think, look and listen within the good company of other writers' (Pirrie, 1993: 16), both from the published page and from the writing community around them in the classroom. I have wanted young writers, through regular exposure to poetry or poetic language, to tune in to what Seamus Heaney (2002: 18) has called 'verbal music' that 'beds' the ear with 'a kind of linguistic hardcore'; to hear what Ted Hughes (1963) has called 'the song and the dance in the words' and to retain what Charles Causley (1989: 7) has called the 'ring in the mind'.

Making Poetry with Children

What follows are snapshots of teaching during which I worked alongside children in a range of classrooms, sharing my experiences of literature, particularly poetry, and helping them to 'find words that will unlock the doors of all those many mansions inside the head' (Hughes, 1967: 124).

At the beginning of one new school year, I became the teacher of a Year 5 class that I had taught in Year 3. I therefore knew something of their reading histories and how they had, at 8 years old, not only become familiar with a wide range of texts and writers but had become apprentice poets in their own right. Now, at 10 years, their literacy skills were honed and their powers of discrimination sharpened.

During a daily session in which children took turns to recommend a book or a writer, a child showed us a book her grandmother had given her with the frontispiece dedication:

> Starlight star bright,
>
> The first star I see tonight
>
> I wish I may
>
> I wish I might
>
> Have the wish I wish tonight.

After she had read us the verse, we talked about the nature of wishes and hopes and of how such longings could be single and attainable or wild and impossible. I read them Robert Frost's poem 'Choose Something Like a Star' and we discussed its sense of wistfulness and the poem's complexities. In groups we looked at copies of Dyan Sheldon's and Gary Blythe's picture book *The Whales' Song (1991)*.

Familiar with Sandy Brownjohn's handbooks for teachers, I drew on her writing starter idea 'I should like…'. We formed writing groups of eight children and within these each child constructed a one line wish and made this his or her contribution to a group poem. Having considered the eight or so single line offerings, the groups discussed ways in which their poem should be structured and came to an agreed running order of lines, a title and ideas for an accompanying illustration. Somewhat eclectic in focus, the finished results nevertheless represented and celebrated the participation of each child. Brownjohn reminds us that 'with all the barriers down and the constraints of the real world forgotten, children are free to experiment' (Brownjohn, 1984: 18).

Armed with the confidence of having subscribed to the group effort, over the next few days children felt able to work on individual poems on this theme of wishing and hoping. The boy whose poem is printed below and whose father had died earlier in the year, seems to have drawn on his raw experience of death and its mystery, expressing his sadness through beautifully measured language. Alongside the poem he drew a whale breaking the surface of a sea:

I should like to hold the soul of the world,

to feel the spirit of the earth.

I should like to hear the heart beats

of the millions who have roamed our planet.

I should like to see the land of the dead

and have knowledge of such things.

I should like to hold the souls of the unliving.

So very different from this wistful articulation of loss, another child expressed herself in a more versified imaginative form:

I should like to twirl with a whirlwind

Wear one of Saturn's rings

Play on the point of a pyramid

Find a Pegasus wing

Float inside a bubble

Hold the breeze in my hand

Dance beneath Australia

Walk the songlines of its land.

Speak the poem of nature

Taste a daffodil grow

Smell the strike of lightning

Feel the warmth of snow.

Robert Frost's poems specifically written for children had their place in the classroom but unexpectedly it was the more complex 'adult' poem about neighbourly relationships, 'Mending Wall', which provoked reflective thought and, surprisingly, for a while, became a regular prompt for general discussion. Its opening lines 'Something there is that doesn't love a wall' intrigued this class and we used that form of words as a kind of linguistic template in order to open up discussions on themes of individual interest or concern. At around this time, as part of a school initiative, we visited a wildlife park and, in preparation, read and discussed a range of poetry linked to animals in their natural world and in captivity ('The Tyger', William Blake; 'India', W.J. Turner; 'The Greater Cats', Vita Sackville-West; 'How to Paint a Portrait of the Bird', Jacques Prevert; 'The Fish', Elizabeth Bishop). Following the visit, strong feelings on the subject of animals in captivity were aired and articulated. Capitalising on this fervour and with Pirrie's (1988: 70) belief that 'the aesthetic experience of writing sharpens and focuses the moral issues more effectively than any amount of didactic teaching', I encouraged the children to express their ideas in written form and through artwork. Recently familiar with the Frost poem, some decided to frame their thoughts around his 'Something there is ...' opening. Here is one child who used this prompt for her comment about a caged jaguar:

> Something there is that isn't right
>
> Iron bars don't match the spotted coat
>
> Don't suit the large cat
>
> This dreaming machine, just pacing.

Here's another expression of discomfort about the idea of animals living in captivity and far from their natural habitat. The writer's decision to express the zebra's need for freedom, albeit local to its surroundings, through unpunctuated language is effective in this case:

> Something there is that doesn't love a cage.
>
> Like this motionless zebra,
>
> melancholy between bars
>
> longing to join the free herd
>
> who gallop today in an English meadow
>
> far from their homeland
>
> filling the distance with a mass
>
> Of black and white.

Interestingly, this theme of captivity was taken up by a child who felt confined in the classroom. Choosing to open her poem in her own way, she likened her school self to that of the caged animals she had observed. She called her poem 'School Room':

> Weekend freedom disappears.
>
> In the captivity of school
>
> our teacher rules the room.
>
> I gaze helplessly beyond the window.
>
> Outside my prison bars
>
> birds fly freely,
>
> clouds move so carelessly
>
> across a summer sky
>
> whilst I stare at figures
>
> captured inside the page.

As an offshoot of this focus on themes of captivity, Elizabeth Bishop's 'The Fish' (1982), which recounts in graphic detail the poet's experience of catching a 'tremendous' fish, provided us with a rich source for word study and oral discussion. With Bishop's evocative, detailed layering of closely observed description and human response to the heroism of the veteran fish, the poem lent itself to being dismantled into constituent sections, each with its own possibility for visual representation. As a class we decided how the poem should be segmented so that pairs of children could take a few self contained lines and convey through artwork a representation of 'their' words. When all the illustrations were complete, we re-assembled the poem around the classroom walls in pictorial sequence and with accompanying scripts.

Children with Special Educational Needs

Ever since a child with Special Educational Needs (SEN), invited to describe herself in one sentence, wrote 'people think I have no imagination but that's where I really live', I have been conscious of the need to provide opportunities for 'less able' children to express themselves through language. This child who lived in her imagination followed up her declaration a few days later with:

> My teacher thinks I'm reading
>
> but sometimes I'm sitting on a cloud
>
> painting the leaves
>
> moving on the trees
>
> or maybe curled up small
>
> inside an empty sea shell
>
> hearing and feeling the waves
>
> bashing against the sides.

Jill Pirrie, in the chapter that gave its name to her first book, writes of the 'common ground' inhabited by children of all abilities. Her belief is that:

[t]he common humanity we share implies a common wavelength of literacy and we should not make the kind of concessions to the less able which exclude them from this wavelength ... many less able children have a natural affinity with poetry ... They experience the relief that few words are required, and the security provided by structure and pattern ... in their writing there is often a refreshing directness and simplicity of expression which a more intelligent child has to struggle to achieve. (Pirrie, 1988: 80)

The wisdom and significance of Pirrie's words was caught for me one day working with small boys in a Special School whose need for support lay in the emotional and behavioural category. Each morning we shared a poem and, for pleasure and reward at the end of an afternoon, listened to Brian Patten and Roger McGough reading from their tape compilation *Jelly-Pie* (1987). In this Early Years group was a child whose language problems were severe and who rarely attempted speech. One afternoon, having indicated that he would like to stand outside in the rain, he came back into the classroom and typed the following:

> The birds are quiet
>
> My skin dribbles
>
> The rain drops.

The two poems below are by children from another school and another classroom whose needs were special, but not as profoundly serious as that particular boy. Matthew Grenby, referring to the work of contemporary poets, speaks of Jackie Kay's work as being 'poetry of the street, or the playground, about real children and their real concerns.... it is not jokey or ephemeral' (Grenby, 2008: 55). Kay's poetry is engaging and readily communicable to children of all abilities but perhaps more so to those who struggle with language. In a Year 5 class, friendships are often under pressure and articulating those tensions is a useful means of diffusing such energy. Kay's collection *Two's Company* (1992) expresses the tensions and strains of friendships and the poem 'Big Hole' (in so far as is possible) takes the child's point of view.

The gentle poignancy of Kay's poem was picked up by a child whose educational needs were indeed special and it was particularly gratifying to read how she worked her own 'twist' into her poem:

> My best friend is quietness
>
> I hold her hand
>
> she talks no louder than a whisper
>
> quietness helps me read
>
> quietness helps me sleep
>
> quietness helps me work.
>
> But quietness is very shy
>
> so when my friends
>
> ask me to play
>
> softly and silently
>
> she slips away

Another pupil of similar ability related to the loneliness Jackie Kay conveys:

I'm lonely, I've been shut off
The Separator has struck again
I'm one side of an invisible wall
It divides us so
no-one can see through.
I can't communicate
I'm lonely, I'm shut off
The Separator has struck again.

Exploring a Theme

In that same class, before we began a science unit on Light, I wanted to explore the theme in literature and introduced Walter de la Mare's poem 'Dream Song' hoping it would provide a model for writing. Unlike Kay's 'Big Hole', the poem, in characteristic de la Mare style, is essentially one that delights in and depends upon a precise rhythmic and rhyming structure, beginning: 'Sunlight, moonlight/Twilight, starlight – /Gloaming at the close of day' (de la Mare, 1946: 103).

It was an ideal choice because the strict form focused pupils' thoughts on echoing the model in a way that made sense. Here's one example:

Candlelight, matchlight
Starlight, daylight
Merging at the close of day,
Birds sleeping
Badgers creeping
Shadows hide their scuttling prey.

And another:

Dawn-light, half-light
Fire-light, storm-light
Gleaming at the close of night
Cats prowling
Foxes howling
Under a sky that's starry bright.

This theme of light and darkness provided much material for creativity. Alan Garner's *The Stone Book* (1999), with its brilliantly evocative description of Mary with her candle going under Glaze Hill and into a sense of her ancestors' presences, provided a focus for thought and communal response. In contrast, we shared Martin Waddell and Barbara Firth's *Can't You Sleep, Little Bear?* (1988), spent time discussing Philip Hobsbaum's poem 'With Half an Eye', read the story of Helen Keller, listened to the 'Adagio' from the Rodrigo *Concierto de Aranjuez*, and thought about living in a world with no external vision. One afternoon I lit candles on tables around which groups of children were sitting and we observed, discussed, and contributed phrases, single words, impressions. Here are two of the immediate observations and poems that were triggered by the study of candlelight:

The Candle of Hope

The light of hope
seems to flicker in one thin flame.
Wax forms a skin like jelly
around the crinkled rim
of the white cylinder.
It will slither and slide then
drop, building a wax barrier
at the candle base.
The burning top is a crater
black wick protruding from its centre
Liquid wax forms in the crater
Only to overflow
Speeding down the waxy cylinder
Reaching the base,
Extending the barrier a little more.

The Demon Flame

A wicked point of light
pierces the air
stretching to reach some highest dream
then stooping to the lowest death.
Grabbing oxygen in its fiery claws
it flares demon curses
at demon songs
thrashing wildly to break loose
from the waxy ground.

This next poem, simply called 'Candle', was written by another girl with a statement of Special Educational Needs. She was an isolated child appearing to have few friends:

A candle flickers.

Standing upright in a dark room.

An owl sits on the window ledge.

In a dark corner there is a girl

who looks at the candle.

She sees the flame is a sharp, hot thistle.

She watches liquid wax running down

Like thickened water.

Katherine Paterson's *Bridge to Terabithia* (1977), Natalie Babbitt's *Tuck Everlasting* (1975), the *Legend of Gilgamesh* (Zeman, 1995) and Susan Varley's picture book *Badger's Parting Gifts* (1985) formed a literary backdrop for a writing focus on loss and endings that was also linked to these earlier ideas of light and dark. The writers of the two poems that follow, interpreting the literature in terms of their own lives, expressed deep feelings in very personal ways. The first example is a poem by a boy whose grandfather had recently died and who had found it impossible to tell anyone of his terrible sense of loss and guilt. Inscrutable in parts, it nevertheless expresses something of the sadness, misunderstood responses and the terrible regret associated with the death of a grandparent. In fact the poem became a channel through which the child's mother could communicate with the boy:

My Grandfather

In the dark gloomy room of my life

Another strong candle had burned

Showing me the way

Past a towering, triumphant rock

That blocked my path.

I was too busy

Finding my way past the rock

To notice my only hope

Flicker and start to fade.

Why didn't I show him I cared?

He was ever loving and caring.

The following poem came out of a sadness associated with a marriage break-up and the clearing of a house. Again, this was a child whose abilities had, until the writing of this piece, been understated:

The Teddy Bear

An old, worn down teddy bear

Sits on a shelf in our attic.

There are holes in his feet and paws,

An old chain hangs round his neck

With a heart dangling from it.

His dress is made from parachute silk,

Was white, but now is turning cream.

Bits float down to the floor

As time passes him by in the attic.

Using Literature and Art

The finely crafted work of children's writers provides inspiration for the writing of children. It has become clear to me how acquaintance with such literature inevitably finds its echoes and radiance in children's own writing. Like Jill Pirrie, Margaret Meek, in her seminal text on the interrelatedness of reading and writing, has convincingly demonstrated how experiences of literature, richly imparted and discerningly interrogated, can seep into the creative impulses and sensitivities of young readers and sound resonances in their own writing. She maintains: 'If we want to see what lessons have been learned from texts children read, we have to look for them in what they write (Meek, 1988: 38).

Ted Hughes, in *Poetry in the Making* (1986: 18) exhorts young writers to 'Imagine what you are writing about. See it and live it'. He encourages children to be detailed (sometimes microscopic) in their observations – to be precise and honest in observation and word and to infuse all perceptions with a personal, first-hand guarantee. With the echoes of good literature in their heads, supported by 'the good company of other writers' children can call on rich well-springs of creativity in order to paint pictures in words. The following three poems were inspired by fine art or evocative photographs of landscapes. The writers were urged to be 'precise and honest' in observation.

The first example, by a child who has found a language for looking closely, is called 'The Vale'. He chose a wide-angled photograph of a small rural village in North Yorkshire, taken in Spring though there is snow on the ground:

The moors unfold
Odd indentations in the landscape
Look like crumpled paper.
The drystone walls around this sleeping village
Break up the lushness of early grass.
Barriers of trees shelter stony homes.
Sheep stray like earthed clouds.
A lapse in time, ageless.

The next poem was inspired by a photograph of a rainbow:

In the yellowness of late evening
this whole hillside is lit with colour.
A rainbow curves, lighting up fields
flickering the windows of houses
that burrow in the hills.
The ribbon of colour climbs up like a plane
then steps over the edge of the world.

A copy of a Dame Laura Knight painting called *In the Fields* was chosen as a subject by a girl. It shows two young women in elaborate Edwardian clothes and another similarly dressed but with a parasol, facing them. It is high summer and the day is clearly hot and the atmosphere enervating. Beyond the figures and the fields is the glint of sea. This girl called her poem 'Companions in a Summer Field':

The summer sun shines down
high clouds are white fleeced.
The sea sparkles in such summer light.

Beneath our feet the grass is wetly soft
Our shoes are sprayed in dew
A light breeze ruffles our hair
And our deep shadows
follow us along the grass.
We are so hot
Our stockings cling to our skin.
The thick heat is held in the clothes we wear.
Time seems stilled and no wind blows.

Conclusions

There is no doubt in my mind that children invest in a teacher's enthusiasm for his or her subject. Helping children find their writing voice through sharing experiences of literature, music, fine art and good discussion, supports their potential for 'saying what [they] really mean'. As teachers we must kindle in young writers a love of words, an appreciation of all language forms in order for them to recognise not only the kinship between literature and literacy but the transforming power of poetry. John Agard suggests that in revealing the extraordinary within the ordinary, poets perform little acts of alchemy: the familiar is seen in a new light. Poets, he says, 'deal with epiphanies' (Agard, 1994). Charles Causley believed that 'poetry is magic ... a spell against insensitivity, ignorance and barbarism' (1974: 15), further stating that 'a poem should be a kind of magic stone that gives out signals' (1989: 16).

Throughout my years in primary school classrooms I saw the magic, the epiphanies, the acts of alchemy, the ordinary rendered extraordinary at the hands of young poets. On the walls of my various classrooms I displayed a poem by Gerda Mayer called 'Shallow Poem'. It captures beautifully, in its image of a milk-filled saucer, the idea that so ordinary a household utensil can serve as a kind of crucible:

> I've thought of a poem.
>
> I carry it carefully,
>
> nervously, in my head,
>
> like a saucer of milk;
>
> in case I should spill some lines
>
> before I can put it down. (In Nicholls, 1988: 86)

The Greek roots of the word poetry are 'to make' or 'to fashion'. Recalling Anne Stevenson's manifesto poem 'Making Poetry', as teachers we must be mindful that the making of poetry is a fragile and vulnerable process – as fragile and vulnerable as the girl who, in an earlier quoted poem, sat with the owl, alone in the dark, watching the 'sharp, hot thistle' of candle flame.

SOMETHING TO THINK ABOUT

In his Introduction to *Tell Me: Children, Reading and Talk*, Aidan Chambers refers to the part that talk plays in the lives of 'discriminating, thoughtful, pleasure-taking readers' (2001: 9). He believes that talking about texts ('booktalk') with other readers is the surest route to gaining insight, understanding and a richer literary experience. How far do you think the maxim 'we don't know what we think about a book until we've talked about it' (p. 15) can be similarly applied to the understanding and appreciation of poetry and to the encouragement of individual creativity? How important is 'poetrytalk' as a stimulus or starting point for writing poetry?

SOMETHING TO READ

Ted Hughes (*Poetry in the Making*), Sandy Brownjohn (*To Rhyme or Not to Rhyme?*), Jill Pirrie (*Apple Fire*) and Michael Rosen (*Did I Hear you Write?*) have all had considerable influence on the teaching of poetry writing, as detailed in the Introduction to this book. Read the work of all four and consider ways you might implement some of their philosophies and practical suggestions in your own classroom practice. Keep up with the regular reviews of poetry books for children in periodicals such as *Carousel* and *Books for Keeps*.

SOMETHING TO DO

A teacher's knowledge of the work of a wide range of poets, a love of poetry and his/her ability to share that enthusiasm with children is fundamental to 'bringing poetry alive' in the classroom, and to the effective teaching of poetry writing. Recent research has suggested that many teachers' knowledge of poetry is limited. Make it a regular practice not only to read poetry for your own enjoyment but to promote within your classroom either the work of a poet or a particular selection of poetry books.

References

Agard, J. (1994) *Poems on the Box*. BBC TV.

Babbitt, N. (1975) *Tuck Everlasting*. New York: Farrar, Strauss & Giroux.

Bennett, A. (2004) *The History Boys*. London: Faber and Faber.

Bishop, E. (1982) 'The Fish', in Heaney, S. and Hughes, T. *The Rattle Bag*. London: Faber and Faber.

Bridges, R. (1953) *Poetical Works of Robert Bridges*. London: OUP.

Brownjohn, S. (1984) *Does it Have to Rhyme?* London: Hodder and Stoughton.

Brownjohn, S. (1994) *To Rhyme or Not to Ryme?* London: Hodder Education.

Causley, C. (1974) (ed.) *The Puffin Book of Magic Verse*. Harmondsworth: Penguin.

Causley, C. (1989) in Merrick, B. *Talking with Charles Causley*. London: National Association for the Teaching of English.

Chambers, A. (2001) *Tell Me: Children, Reading and Talk*. Stroud: Thimble Press.

Church, R. (1955) *Over the Bridge: An Essay in Autobiography*. London: Heinemann.

de la Mare, W. (1946) *Peacock Pie*. London: Faber and Faber.

Frost, R. (1973) *Selected Poems*. London: Penguin Books.

Garner, A. (1999) *The Stone Book Quartet*. London: Flamingo.

Grenby, M. (2008) *Children's Literature*. Edinburgh: Edinburgh University Press.

Heaney, S. (2002) *Finders Keepers: Selected Prose 1971–2001*. London: Faber and Faber.

Heaney, S. (2004) *Room To Rhyme*. Dundee: University of Dundee.

Hobsbaum, P. (1964) 'With Half an Eye', in Wollman, M. & Grugeon, D. (eds) *Happenings: New Poems for Junior Schools*. London: Harrap.

Hughes, T. (ed.) (1963) 'Listening to Poetry', *Here Today*. Hutchinson Educational.

Hughes, T. (1967) *Poetry in the Making*. London: Faber and Faber.

Hughes, T. (1986) *Poetry in the Making: An Anthology of Poems and Programmes from 'Listening and Writing'*. London: Faber and Faber.

Kay, J. (1992) *Two's Company*. London: Blackie Children's Books.

Knight, R. (1994) 'Free the Native Spirit', *Times Educational Supplement*, 18 February.

Meek, M. (1988) *How Texts Teach What Readers Learn*. Stroud: The Thimble Press.

Newbolt, H.J. (1921) *The Teaching of English in England* (The Newbolt Report). London: HM Stationery Office.

Nicholls, G. (1988) *Wordspells*. London: Faber and Faber.

Paterson, K. (1977) *Bridge to Terabithia*. London: Puffin Books.

Patten, B. & McGough, R. (1987) *Jelly-Pie*. Cover to Cover Cassettes Ltd.

Pirrie, J. (1988) *On Common Ground: A Programme for Teaching Poetry*. London: Hodder and Stoughton.

Pirrie, J. (1992) 'Giants, Castles and Moonlit Apples', *Times Educational Supplement*, 8 May.

Pirrie, J. (ed.) (1993) *Apple Fire: The Halesworth Middle School Anthology*. Newcastle on Tyne: Bloodaxe Books.

Sheldon, D. & Blythe, G. (1991) *The Whales' Song*. London: Hutchinson.

Stevenson, A. (2005) *Poems 1955–2005*. Newcastle on Tyne: Bloodaxe Books.

Stevenson, A. & O'Siadhail, M. (1989) 'An Interview with Anne Stevenson', *The Poetry Ireland Review*, 26 (Summer): 6–9. Poetry Ireland.

Varley, S. (1985) *Badger's Parting Gifts*. London: Collins Picture Lions.

Waddell, M. & Firth, B. (1988) *Can't You Sleep, Little Bear?* London: Walker Books.

Wilson, A. (2001) 'Brownjohn, Hughes, Pirrie, and Rosen: What Rhymes with Oral Writing?' London: National Association for the Teaching of English.

Zeman, L. (1995) *The Last Quest of Gilgamesh* (a retelling). Montreal: Tundra Books.

Chapter 5

'Look, Children – a Real, Live Poet!': The Role of the Poet in Primary Schools

James Carter

CHAPTER OVERVIEW

In this chapter, James Carter describes in detail the various kinds of visits he makes to schools in the UK and abroad and reflects on what he encounters there, including one-day visits, in-service training days, and gifted and talented writers' days. He also gives advice on what teachers can do to make the most of such visits by poets, both for themselves and for their pupils. The chapter tries to provide specific answers to the questions: 'Why are poets invited into school?' and 'What are "real live" poets good for?'

Until recently, children's poetry was not in a good state. Fewer and fewer anthologies and collections were being published each year. Now, slowly, there seems to be some recovery; at the time of writing, for example, there are five publishers currently working hard on their poetry lists. However, children's poetry continues not to sell as well as its prose counterparts. Why should this be? Some believe we published and saturated the market with too many titles 10 years ago, and, on top of this, there seems to be a finite market for verse. Others argue that it reflects the fact that much of what is published is performance poetry that works best in a live context. This could indeed be part of a bigger issue – that we, the book-buying public, would rather watch poets live than read their work on the page. Some critics and reviewers have been quite vocal in stating that there has been too much of an emphasis on 'funny' poetry in recent years, and thus people aren't taking children's poetry seriously as a literary medium and hence don't buy it. As a result, a number of children's poets have to self-publish to support their work in schools.

Poetry publishing lists have also been affected by the fact that some bigger names, such as Roger McGough, Brian Patten, Allan Ahlberg and Benjamin Zephaniah, are currently not writing and publishing as much poetry for children as previously. Some publishers say that they won't touch poetry any longer because 'it doesn't sell', and yet will happily continue to put marketing muscle into fiction and non-fiction. Is this because they have more confidence in these areas? Or does it reflect a genuine difficulty in selling books of verse?

At ground level, children's – and indeed adult's – poetry is arguably more popular than ever. Performers and poets who run workshops are in high demand in schools, libraries and at the many literary festivals around the UK – particularly around the two polar points of the school year, World Book Day (the first Thursday in March) and National Poetry Day (the first Thursday in October). I estimate that there are some several hundred of us 'real live poets' regularly walking the boards of primary schools. Some of these poets are high-profile names, some not so well known, some not even published at all, but simply great with words and at getting children switched on to writing. Whatever the poet's status, children need to see that poems are written by everyday people who simply have a talent for using and crafting language, and a love of sharing it with others, for demythologising the writing process, and for encouraging others into 'the word thing'.

But do children like poetry? Actually they love it! That's the conclusion I've come to having worked as a writer-in-schools for over eight years. I can feel the excitement when I visit a school that another poet has just been to. Children are buzzing with it – and they seem to relish reading, writing, performing and even watching my many colleagues come in and do their poetry shows. I would add that primary teachers, in the main, seem to really love it too, and appreciate the value of poetry on and off the page and across the primary curriculum.

So, why is it that a great many adults claim that poetry is either 'boring', 'difficult' or 'academic'? Where does this all stem from? My theory is that something goes wrong at secondary school level. This is no reflection on the teachers, for I have observed a lot of very dynamic and creative teaching in English Departments at secondary level. I'm referring to the system that starts analysing and deconstructing poetry in preparation for GCSEs. That's when students go off poetry, and maddeningly, frustratingly, this negative response seems to remain through adulthood. Generally speaking, as far as I can gauge, the average person seems to dislike deconstructing text. Poetry is a prime target for deconstruction because of its brevity. So this may be one of the main reasons why poetry in general is so much more readily dismissed than any other literary form. What would be a revealing exercise would be to do a survey on children's attitudes towards poetry in all the year groups in primary as well as secondary, such as those by the Assessment of Performance Unit (APU) carried out in the late 1970s and 1980s (see APU, 1988).

Throughout the school term, I visit a great many primary schools (as well as a number of libraries and book festivals) to do poetry performances and workshops. I take my guitar along as it's fun to play; it seems to focus the children and also serves to highlight the musicality of language. I tell teachers that my job is the antithesis of theirs: they have a rolling curriculum with the same children all year round, whereas I do poetry, always poetry, every day – but in four different schools, every week.

If I'm to be honest, the success of a day depends very much upon the teachers. Children are always fantastic – they're usually responsive and keen to enjoy some musical language. But it's how the teachers approach and frame the day and 'big up' that experience for the children that really counts. On those days when the children have done research on my work at my website, prepared some questions, maybe even worked up a performance of one of my poems for me, the experience couldn't be better. Everyone gets so much out of the day. Only very occasionally – maybe once every two years, if that – I'll feel that I'm simply there to tick a box and so that the school can tell Ofsted they had a poet in. On those days, the teachers mark as I am performing and workshopping, and even chat amongst themselves (or worse still, leave the room), though I'm too cheeky a visitor to let that happen for any length of time!

Visits to schools tend to fall into three types: a one-day visit, an in-service training (INSET) day, and a gifted and talented writers' day.

A One-day Visit

Most school visits are for one day. Once or twice a term, I'll do a two-day visit, and once or so a year I'll take on a residency, either for a number of weeks, or across a term or even across the academic year. On a single day visit, I'll probably work with and meet each child in the school at least twice. For example, between 9am and 3.30pm I will do:

- A KS2 assembly in the hall
- A KS1 assembly in the hall
- A visit to the Reception class(es)
- Poetry writing workshops, using rhyme and free verse
- Poetry Finale in the hall (with parents invited)
- Bookselling/signing

It's quite an intense and intensive day, but I want to achieve a lot, in terms of both performances and workshops. I separate out KS2 and KS1 as fundamentally, for me at least, they are two very different audiences. With KS2,

I will do a whole range of material, but it tends to begin with gentle instrumental guitar music then five or so quieter, more reflective poems (free and rhyming verse on all kinds of topics from wolves to love to angels); then for the second half, I 'crank it up', play some wilder guitar music and do some comic, quirky material.

Key Stage 2

Long gone are the days when a poet could stand at the front of the hall, shuffle a few manuscript pages around and open up with 'Good morning, children. I'm going to read you some new poems. Who can tell me what a poem is?' Children – particularly KS2 – expect to be entertained. So, the new breed of children's poets uses instruments – guitars, drums, percussion, ukuleles and so forth – as well as props and costumes. Some do magic tricks and juggle. One, Matt Black, even has a Poetry Juke Box that he takes around schools and libraries. Poets do many things to keep these 7–11-year-olds entertained. They move around the hall. They invite children up to read, to chant, to get involved, and to partici-pate. Some do stand-up comedy between poems. They get children to clap along, impersonate things, and join in during the choruses.

For most contemporary children's poets, it's not simply a question of reading but performing a poem. There is a significant difference. It's not just a matter of decoding the words and reading them with some meaning. Most poets nowa-days know most of the poems they perform off by heart. This is essential if you are going to bring the thing to life. And in a performance, a poet will do this with a range of tools available – actions, gestures, pauses, eye contact – and use varying pitch, timbre, and emphases. It's not as easy as it seems and some poets cannot do it at all; they would rather leave it to others. I find it takes two months plus to work a new poem into my 'set', where I know it off by heart, know that I'm saying and meaning and delivering each word, phrase and line as I feel it should be. This is a real creative challenge, giving a poem a second life, one off the page. On top of this, I have to do it in a way that will engage a child audience. The most wonderful compliment I have received was from a KS2 boy who told me: 'it's like we are inside the poem with you'. That has become the benchmark by which to evaluate each new piece I work on. Also, not every poem works as a 'live' poem. Many poems that I write, I have discovered, are strictly 'page poems' and would rather be read quietly in the mind's ear.

Key Stage 1 and Reception

A KS1 performance, for me, couldn't be more different from a KS2 one. For 5–7-year-olds, I used to do a diluted version of my KS2 'set', but found it didn't work. In a performance, funny material is problematic with Years 1 and 2 as they can get excited very quickly, and it can take a while to calm them down.

As teachers repeatedly tell me, if you do funny material the children start laughing and stop listening.

Because of this, I will do quiet but engaging and interactive poems through-out, and end with something a little more lively. The poems will be about all kinds of subjects: bears, bubbles, travelling around the world, dinosaurs, pirates. I do a lot of actions, because Infants love joining in with these. At various points I'll play some very gentle instrumental guitar music, and encourage the children to have imaginative responses to what I'm playing, and then I'll ask children up to talk about their ideas. I take my writing for this age group as seriously as I do for any other. It's more of a challenge to write poems for the under-7s, keeping the poems fun, stimulating, age-appropriate and using rhythmical language and a slightly more restricted and direct vocabulary, without being twee, sentimental or trite, but it's very rewarding.

For Reception classes, I actually go and visit the classroom and show them my picture book, *Around the World* (2007a). With every page I'll invite responses from the children, and from there we'll do a few action rhymes, and possibly some riddle poems about minibeasts. Less is always more with rising 5s. But interestingly, I find that as the academic year progresses, this age group can sustain a poetry session for much longer, even half an hour, which is a long time with material they have never come across before. Unless I'm in an Infant school, I tend not to visit age-groups below Reception as I can only do a finite number of sessions in one day and I only have a finite amount of energy!

Generally, as regards the material I choose to use in KS2, KS1 or Reception performances, children deserve a diet of more than just funny rhymes. As poets, it is our role to demonstrate the variety of poetry, both in terms of forms or modes and in terms of voices, tones and subject matters. We should be using poetry as a vehicle to tell stories – real or imagined – to explore the world and the world of ideas, to express our emotions, to shock, delight, fascinate, enlighten, educate, empathise and intrigue. I despair when I hear from teachers of poets doing half an hour to an hour in the school hall of just funny rhymes. Of course we are there to entertain, but many other things besides.

Poetry Writing Workshops

Once the KS2, KS1 or Reception performances are out of the way, I will begin the workshops. After morning break, it will be time to visit three or four single classrooms to do poetry writing workshops. More often than not, depending on the size of the school, it will be four KS2 classes. Occasionally, a school will ask me to do a workshop only with the KS1 classes, which I am more than happy to do. Sometimes teachers ask me to cover a specific topic. This can work well, but only if I know I have a poetic form or structure that will serve the subject well. Otherwise, I will stick to the range of workshops that I know get good results. The workshops I do include kennings, raps, rhyming verse, calligrams and all kinds of different free verse models and forms. However in the main, I use free verse, as schools tend to work through each of the popular poetic forms (e.g. haikus, tankas, limericks) and there's nothing worse than when halfway through a workshop someone asks the teacher, 'Oh, didn't we do this last week, Miss?'

The first poem that follows was created in a workshop in a large, urban primary school in Oxfordshire. For me, this 'Animal Rhyme' workshop is good for developing rhythm and rhyme. It helps children to explore simple imagery, and encourages them to find descriptive adjectives and verbs associated with animals. Once finished, I ask the class to think of actions to accompany the poem. When performed in the Poetry Finale assembly at the end of the day, often half the class will say the words and the other half do the actions.

Animal Rhyme

Happy as a hippo
swimming in the lake
cheeky as a monkey
sneaky as a snake

Timid as a turtle
shuffling on the shore
scary as a tiger
letting out a roar

Spotty as a ladybird
stripey as a bee
pretty as a butterfly
itchy as a flea

Fiery as a dragon
soaring through the sky
these were the animals…
say goodbye!

(Year 1 Classes, Ladygrove Park Primary School)

From there, I show the class my poetry books. There are many things I might choose to discuss at this point. I might talk about assembling an anthology, and putting together a collection. I might discuss titles and covers, and why I have chosen to do certain topics for books, such as science, space and the natural world. I might show them my shape poems and talk about how I write and design them. I always talk about the writing of a poem – I show a working draft and tell each class that a poem can take up to six months to write. This, for me – showing a draft, and talking about the decision-making process, the moving around of stanzas, the varying titles a poem might have during the process, the need for a strong opening and a satisfying conclusion, the need for flow and structure, the need for tightness and scansion, the honing in on each and every single word in a poem – is probably the most important part of the day. Children need to see that writing is a craft skill. It is at this point that the class will frequently ask questions about publishing and the process of writing. To the perennial 'Where do you get your ideas from?' I tell them literally 'anywhere', and talk through the evolution of a couple of specific poems.

The actual workshop I choose depends on a number of things: the age of the class, their ability overall (as signalled by the teacher), what poetry they have done during the term or year, as well as how responsive they seem as a group. I love taking the children's words and ideas and moulding them into a coherent shape as a class poem on the board. Children need to see and appreciate the randomness of ideas and thoughts, the trial and error of it all, that perhaps we'll write the stanzas out of sequence then move them all around, or that we'll have to keep coming back to the third line until it flows and says exactly what we want it to. They need to see the blood, sweat and tears that can go into the simplest lines, just to get it right. I'm quite tough on a class; I won't tell them an idea is good if I don't think it is. I aim to be supportive but positively critical. Overall, I need to recreate in their class a microcosm of the writing process – an intense, intensive 30-minute version of the many months that I work on a poem, with the multiplicity of chops and changes, edits and re-writes and tweaks along the way.

Rhyme

Some poets seem to avoid using rhyme in workshops with children. Until recently I did the same, though I've now come to the conclusion that children need to be shown how to rhyme effectively. From birth onwards, we give children lullabies, nursery rhymes, nonsense rhymes, and rhymes in picture books. Then around the age of 7 children are told by a teacher that 'not all poetry rhymes'. We give children seven years of rhyme, through the Foundation Stage and KS1 and then in KS2 we try and stop them writing it themselves. Actually, children are not great at writing rhyme. They don't have the extended vocabularies yet, as well as the patience and the experience to know that writing a random series of rhymes is not a poem. However, rhyming is not as difficult as rhythm; a rhyming poem will, by its nature, have a rhythmical pattern, and this area is difficult enough for adults to fully grasp, let alone children at KS1 or KS2.

How many times have you come across this type of writing from a child?

> I went to the beach
> I sat on a peach
> I tried to teach
> I saw a ... leech?

As the poet Valerie Bloom says, rhyme is like fire, and you need to be in control of it, it must not be in control of you (Bloom, 2000).

Without doubt, free verse is the best poetic medium for children to explore and express their own experiences, thoughts and imaginings, as well as for all the cross-curricular work that goes on at KS2. However, children want to rhyme at times and they should be allowed to. To improve their rhyming and rhythmical skills, they need to practise rhymes out of context, using both full rhymes, for example:

> I've got a friend
>
> her name is Ruth
>
> she loves to wiggle
>
> her wobbly tooth

and also, at KS2, half rhymes, such as:

> I've got a friend
>
> her name is Kim
>
> she loves to play
>
> the violin.

The more practice with rhyme the better, though my feeling is that time spent with rhyming dictionaries is counter-productive: it interrupts the creative flow and leads to children spending excessive time flicking through dictionaries to find out what all the rhyming words mean.

If children start to rhyme in a free verse workshop, I will most probably try and persuade them to take the rhymes out, and will offer them alternative phrases. Yet, there are times when children are using rhyme confidently, and I will encourage them to continue. Children need to know that you cannot be overly dogmatic about creative writing, there needs to be room for flexibility and allowing an idea to take the shape it wants to. Sometimes children begin to write prose in a free verse workshop, and that's fine, as there is often a blurring between free verse and prose.

One major concern I have as I look around each classroom is that the current curriculum seems over-preoccupied with deconstruction. I believe that too much analysis and dissection of text at this stage in a child's learning will not help creative writing at all and will certainly not switch on any of those reluctant readers or writers. I call this over-deconstructive approach not creative but 'destructive writing'. An over-prescriptive approach makes children anxious about their writing. Surely, what we need is for children to feel free and uninhibited. My analogy for the creative and deconstructive approaches is this: when you are learning to drive a car do you expect the instructor to show you a detailed diagram of the engine, explaining where the spark plugs are? The same applies to writing: you just get on with it, and all that technical stuff can come later.

⬤ Free Verse

Below is an exceptional free verse poem, written during the Ledbury Festival in 2009, by a then Year 4 girl. The workshop which inspired this was loosely based on one by the writer Fred Sedgwick called 'Gifts', and this was the second time I had tried it out.

Impossible Gifts

(for Grace)

These are the gifts
that I would if I could
give to you …

The moon wrapped in the pull of
a magnet,
a bucket of stars mixed
with the softest cloud,
an angel's heart sewn to a rainbow
cloak.

I would give to you …
the ring of hope placed on the invisible
hand of God,
the force of gravity wound around
the first snowflake to fall,
the speed of light bundled up in
a scarlet sky.

I would give to you …
the song of a bee drowned
by the loudest battle cry,
the laugh of a baby hidden
in the depths of the River Nile,
the sting of a jellyfish
trapped in the bluest sea.

I would give to you …
the tear of a phoenix buried in
the chest of a griffin,

the prick of a needle encrusted

in the crown of King Arthur.

These are the gifts I would

if I could give to you.

(Isobel Owen)

Clearly Isobel has much experience of writing free verse, she has a vast imagination and has a grasp of language well beyond her years. What is also apparent is that Isobel reads a great deal. Teachers and parents frequently ask me how to raise the standard of writing, and all I can recommend is to work on the reading first. Great writers are great readers. When I interviewed Malorie Blackman, Jacqueline Wilson and Philip Pullman in their homes, I could hardly move for books.

'Impossible Gifts' is not a workshop I do regularly, but when I do use it, I find the quality of writing is particularly high, perhaps because I have asked them to address the poem to someone they are very fond of, so the words they write are more heartfelt. With this workshop I insist that the class include only elements that are impossible. I give them a list of areas as prompts: something ancient; from the past or future; a smell or a sound; something opposite; something from the sea or space; the five senses – a smell, a sound and so on. Teachers will note the workshop itself is not dissimilar to the ever popular 'The Magic Box' by Kit Wright (1987), and likewise, is great for imagery and expressive language.

Poet and anthologist John Foster comments:

As teachers we should present poems as models. I believe the way to develop people as writers is to present them with a text and to analyse it, to look at what the writer is doing and the techniques that the writer is employing in that particular text. Then, the children can have a go at writing in the same way – not using the same content, but the techniques and the appropriate form. Then comes the stage that so often is missed, which is for the children to analyse where they have succeeded or not. This is not for the teacher to do, but for the children – and for them to look objectively at their own work. Until you start to evaluate your writing critically you can't begin to develop or improve as a writer. (Foster, 2001: 25)

I do use a range of poems as models myself, and adhere to Foster's sentiments. Emulating a form in this way is also effective for helping young writers discover poetic techniques, devices, and a whole gamut of writers' tricks they can employ in their own writing. However, I also strongly believe that, effective as this method is, too much of it can result in formulaic, fill-in-the-gaps writing. This is fine as an exercise, but children do need to find their own voices as well, so ought to be given space to write free verse with their own language and their own structures. In an after school writing club I have been running,

I have found that the very best things that the very mixed ability group of Year 5 and 6 children have produced is when the stabilisers are off, and I push aside the 'workshop structures', simply giving them an opening phrase or playing them some instrumental music and letting them have *carte blanche* to write whatever they like. The results have been fantastic. They especially enjoy writing to music, exploring their creativities, and discovering new ways of expressing themselves. Children need – and respond well to – this kind of freedom.

Here's one such piece, a first draft of a poem by a very talented young writer, whose imagery is fresh, striking and most unusual. This poem was inspired by some North-African style music from my CD and book *Just Imagine* (2002):

Flashes of my Broken Dreams

Flashes of my broken dreams

That I never achieved

Very tiny little things

That I will always read

Things that I might write about

That might not be true

Like seeing things impossible

Or staying here with you

Broken bones and blackened skin

Things I lost before

Things that I don't think about

Like my heart in a drawer.

(Jack Brown)

As educationalist Pie Corbett rightly states:

We have to develop children as creative, innovative writers. We do not want classes full of automatons that fill in gaps and do exactly what you tell them to do. But at times, this is the way that children learn to write. So it's a fine balance. Children need opportunities to do both. (Corbett, 2009: 6)

There are a number of key issues I need to get across in a workshop:

- For a first draft, anything goes. You have to be uninhibited and feel free to write anything that comes to you.
- In a poem, every single word counts. I tell children I can spend up to 20 minutes just changing a single syllable or word.
- Anyone can write a poem.

- A poem takes time. Don't expect a first draft to be perfect. Just relax. Write something. See what happens.
- Writing is great fun – but needs a fair bit of effort, though it's well worth it.

The poetry performance in the hall and the poetry writing workshops in the classrooms serve similar but related functions. The performance in the hall is all about engaging the young audience, entertaining them, and enlightening them as to what poetry can be when spoken, chanted and sung; brought to life with actions, props or musical instruments. The workshop is about immersing the class in language, but this time allowing them to be actively creative themselves, to try out a new form, to develop their skills, to learn more about the craft and the process, to learn how to write economically but expressively in the way that poetry uniquely does, to have fun with words and, above all else, to develop their confidences as writers. Needless to say, confidence for a writer is everything.

Poetry Finale

Increasingly, I will offer a school a Poetry Finale (as I tend to call it) at the end of the visit. This is in the hall, with the whole school and even parents in attendance. It gives the school a final chance to see me do a couple more poems, but far more importantly, four or so volunteers from each of the classes I have workshopped with will come out and read their poems. Most children love doing this. They are beaming with pride and a sense of achievement. And, interestingly, teachers frequently comment to me that those children that shine on a day like this are usually not those who are commonly the highest achievers in Literacy. For me, this is what a day like this should be about – giving the opportunity to those who are not usually in the top set to enjoy, succeed in, and gain confidence in their writing. I often wonder why this should be the case, but I suspect it's because some children are prepared to take risks with their writing with someone that they don't know, who is not going to 'mark' or comment upon their creativity afterwards.

Occasionally, a school will ask me to conduct a series of poetry performance workshops. This will entail choosing a poem (say Lewis Carroll's 'Jabberwocky', Jack Ousbey's 'Gran Can You Rap?', Nick Toczek's 'The Dragon Who Ate Our School', Allan Ahlberg's 'Heard It In The Playground', or even my own poem 'World of Weird') and working with the class not on a reading, but a performance of the poem. We look at individual words, lines and verses. We might break the class into smaller groups to do some verses each. We might choose props, actions, vocal sound effects, even audience participation. We consider volume, pitch, tone, mood, atmosphere, narrative, and other elements. This is a very healthy form of deconstruction, and empowers children to do their own interpretation. The children will learn the poem, keep rehearsing the piece and develop it further with the teacher, performing it in either an assembly or

Poetry Gala later in the week. Again, teachers tell me that those children that excel in this kind of activity will often not be those that usually do well in creative writing.

Children performing and actually learning poems off by heart can have multiple benefits. First, it's all about building confidence, developing performance skills, and beyond this, interpreting text creatively, working and improvising and developing a routine collaboratively as a group. The learning of a poem is fundamental. I would have every child learn at least a dozen poems before they leave primary school. These will serve them well throughout the teenage years and adulthood. We need an internal library, a repertoire of language models, internal rhythms, templates and structures within which to write, to create our own rhythms, our own poems. I wrote my poem 'The Wolf Outside' to the iambic rhythm of a spoken Tom Waits song, but I am only able to do this kind of thing (which, in this case, just occurred naturally during a daydream), because I actively learn whole or even fragments of poems and songs. Granted children will go on to Year 7 knowing a great many songs, but how many poems will they have learned?

Gifted and Talented Writers' Days

One headteacher accused the Gifted and Talented Writers' Days (also known as Able Writers' Days) of being elitist. I think he was missing the point. Teachers often spend a lot of time with the lower and middle achievers at the expense of the higher achievers. This is why such days are vital. I will spend a whole day, frequently with children from a cluster of schools, from both Years 5 and 6. We will be in a classroom, hall or library for the day, and I will have either a teacher or Learning Support Assistant to help me. They're highly intensive days but great fun, and the children, more often than not, seem to raise the bar, simply because you are giving them permission to be great. I will take the group on a journey from simple word-play (Year 6 in particular can often forget about being playful in their writing) to increasingly sophisticated free verse forms – with imagery and metaphor of all kinds – and then we'll finish the day with some Dahlesque, 'Revolting Rhymes'-style raps. The children go home looking a little weary but clutching some wonderful writing.

INSET

I feel that when I come into a school my visit works on two fundamental levels – although I'm primarily there to involve and engage the children, it's also to deliver an implicit in-service training (INSET) session, showing teachers ways that poetry can be delivered, performed, shared, written, modelled and so on. In my actual INSET sessions I do very little chalk and talk, I simply work through a very wide range of poetry and fiction workshops – appropriate for Reception to Year 6 – that teachers can pick up and take straight back to the classroom. The best comment I can get after an INSET session is: 'Great! I've got loads of practical stuff to take back to my classroom – starting tomorrow!'

Poet Tony Mitton (1999: 31) reflects: 'I often feel that the people who do creative writing best with children are teachers'. On one level I feel this is true; teachers do much wonderful creative writing with children, despite the fact that many of them have had little or no real training in this area. Yet contrary to Mitton's sentiment, teachers all over the UK regularly inform me that they themselves very much need to invite poets and all kinds of creative writers into schools, to discover how they write themselves and how they write collaboratively with children. Interestingly, and perhaps tellingly, teachers regularly confess to feeling much more confident in doing prose fiction with children. On top of this, teachers admit they don't take poetry as seriously as story writing. I wholeheartedly agree with Pie Corbett when he says:

> I don't think schools always recognise how important poetry is to children. The people who devise curriculums don't either. Poetry is where you learn how to be a writer – probably even more so than with prose. Because of the brevity of It, it's more achievable. It's where you learn how to play with words, to craft language, to love the words and the ideas expressed in words – and value the power, the pleasure and beauty of words. With poetry you can do all kinds of things – boast, lie, imagine, wonder, wish, hope and dream. (Corbett, 2009: 19)

Is it not easier for children to indulge in all kinds of language play – alliteration, assonance, repetition, rhymes, or free verse – before moving on to the massive leap forward to writing a story? Some teachers have also confessed to me they don't do much poetry because it is not assessed at KS1 or KS2. A big part of me is relieved it is not assessed. I detest the idea of Year 6 children having to knock off a haiku, tanka or cinquain in 20 minutes, so it can then be assessed and graded. If this was the case, there'd be even more resentment towards verse from adults.

Conclusions

Why exactly are we poets invited into schools? Teachers email me with all kinds of reasons: to help them celebrate National Poetry Day, World Book Day, or their Book/Poetry Week. It might be to 'switch on those reluctant boy writers'. It might be to tie in with a topic: 'Come and do Egyptian/Animal/Space/Victorian Poetry'.

It might be to work with one class that has been reading my poems. It might be to do a specific form of poetry with a class. It might be because a teacher has found my website and wants to try out a Poetry Day. It might be to keep Year 6 happy for a day once SATS have finished. It might be to judge a poetry competition, to give both the teachers and the children confidence in either writing or performing, or just 'come in and inspire us!'

I suppose what we poets bring in is expertise, an in-depth knowledge of our subject, but along with that a passion for language and for sharing it with others. I'm acutely aware that primary teachers have to deliver a very wide curriculum and cannot be experts in every subject, and indeed every single aspect of Literacy. The teachers I meet on a daily basis vary greatly. Some are very well versed in verse: they know the classics and the contemporaries and even write their own poems, and maybe even the annual school play and all the songs in it. Others think they know very little, but are doing a great job with an area that is not their specialism at all. At the other end of the spectrum are those that admit to doing very little poetry and call it 'difficult' and 'scary'.

So, to sum up, what is poetry good for?

- looking at language in close-up
- saying a lot in a little
- rubbing words together to see what happens and see what music they'll make
- expressing the inner self, the everyday and the world at large
- exploring all the things that language can be
- telling new and ancient stories
- stomping around and getting rhythmical
- being utterly serious and totally daft
- switching on readers
- switching on writers
- considering possibilities and impossibilities.

And what are 'real live' poets good for?

- setting creativity free
- spreading the word that words are great
- putting on a performance
- showing how poems have a life off the page
- helping to raise the bar
- boosting confidence
- developing craft skills
- showing (certainly not telling) that books are crammed with good stuff
- having a whole lot of fun along the way.

And that, for me, is what we 'real live' poets should be doing – taking in a little bit of all of this into schools all over the country, every day.

SOMETHING TO THINK ABOUT

Children love poetry and respond so readily to it. What can your school do to ensure that poetry is at the heart of the school literacy policy, ensuring that each child has regular poetry experiences – reading, enjoying, discussing, performing and writing poetry?

SOMETHING TO READ

In an ideal world, every Year 6 child would leave primary school knowing at least a dozen poems off by heart. Invite every member of staff – teachers and assistants alike – to read as much children's poetry as they can over a fortnight and, in an informal staff meeting, pick the top 12 poems – modern, classic, quiet or funny ones – that each Year 6 leaver in your school should know. From there, encourage children from the youngest upwards to learn the poems. And why not put on a poetry show?

SOMETHING TO DO

For the next fortnight, set aside five minutes every morning to read a poem to your class. Try poems from different books and from other countries. Try a range of styles, voices and forms – from haikus to raps, from quiet poems to funny ones. At the end of each week, ask the children to vote for their favourite poem. If the class responds well to the 'poem a day', have this as a feature of every school week, every term.

References

Ahlberg, A. (1989) *Heard It in the Playground*. London: Viking Kestrel.

Assessment of Performance Unit (APU) (1988) *Review of APU Language Monitoring 1979–83*. London: HMSO.

Bloom, V. (2000) 'Rhyme Like Fire' [interview with James Carter], *Literacy & Learning*. Birmingham: Questions Publishing.

Carroll, L. (1871) 'Jabberwocky', in *Through the Looking-Glass and What Alice Found There*. London: Macmillan.

Carter, J. (2002) *Just Imagine: Creative Ideas for Writing*. London: David Fulton.

Carter, J. (2007a) *Around the World*. London: HarperCollins.

Carter, J. (2007b) 'World of Weird', in *Time-Travelling Underpants*. London: Macmillan.

Carter, J. (2009) 'The Wolf Outside', in J. Carter & G. Denton (eds) *WILD! Rhymes That Roar*. London: Macmillan.

Corbett, P. (2009) in J. Carter *Creating Writers: A Creative Writing Manual for KS2 & 3*, 2nd edn. London: Routledge.

Dahl, R. (1984) *Revolting Rhymes*. London: Puffin.

Foster, J. (2001) 'Professor of Anthology' [interview with James Carter], *Literacy & Learning*. Birmingham: Questions Publishing.

Mitton, T. (1999) 'Language Dancing' [interview with James Carter], *Literacy & Learning*. Birmingham: Questions Publishing.

Ousbey, J. (2010) 'Gran, Can You Rap?', in J. Foster (ed.) *I've Got a Poem for You*. Oxford: Oxford University Press.

Toczek, N. (1996) *The Dragon Who Ate Our School*. London: Macmillan.

Wright, K. (1987) 'The Magic Box', in *Cat Among the Pigeons*. London: Viking Kestrel.

Chapter 6

Cross-Curricular Poetry Writing

Eileen Hyder

CHAPTER OVERVIEW

This chapter considers ways of using poetry across the curriculum. Using examples from classroom practice and children's work, it shows that the content of other curriculum subjects can provide exciting and dynamic opportunities for writing poetry. In the process, children's understanding of work is consolidated and poetry writing becomes more meaningful. The chapter, therefore, suggests that poetry should not be restricted to the English classroom but used widely across the curriculum.

In the autumn of 2003 I attended a conference led by Sue Palmer and Pie Corbett. As part of this conference, they were introducing their book *Literacy: What Works?* (2003). It was a wonderful day, one of those times when you leave a conference with your mind buzzing with excitement and desperate to get back to school to share and try out new ideas.

For me, one of the most exciting things about the day was the focus on cross-curricular work. The introduction of the National Literacy and Numeracy Strategies meant that time for these subjects was ring-fenced, but the result was that other curriculum areas had to fight over the remaining time. More experienced teachers looked back nostalgically to when things were freer, to when they did project work linking aspects of the curriculum around a theme. Suddenly cross-curricular work became the buzzword – a way of dealing with concerns over the compartmentalisation of the curriculum. I had come into primary teaching at the same time as the National Strategies were being introduced so this was all I knew. Nevertheless, even without a point of comparison, I knew that I often felt frustrated with the work we were doing in some subjects. For example, in my school at that time, History and Geography had 40 minutes a week during alternate half terms. I was always dissatisfied with what we managed to cover. At the *Literacy: What Works?* conference, the focus was on text types. Whether Literacy lessons involved recounts, reports, instructions, explanations, persuasion or discussion, we were shown how the content could be linked to other curriculum areas. The idea was to select a writing objective from the NLS, then identify subject matter in any curriculum area appropriate to that particular text type. All of a sudden I felt liberated. I could read historical reports in Literacy and so cover more of our History topic. Alternatively, we could use the content from a Geography lesson as the focus for our writing in Literacy; this had the advantage of meaning that the children would have plenty of ideas to write about and give the writing more meaning and purpose. It all seemed so obvious.

After the conference, I began to look for cross-curricular links to use in all aspects of Literacy work, not just the non-fiction text types mentioned above but also poetry writing. In fact, it is examples of poetry writing that stick in my memory more than any other type of cross-curricular work. For the purpose of this chapter, I will focus on three examples where poetry writing was linked to other subjects. The examples include work from three different age-groups (Years 5, 7 and 8), come from two different schools and include links to History, Religious Studies and Classics.

History – Ancient Greece

At the time of the conference I was Year 5 class teacher and Literacy Co-ordinator at a local primary school. In History one of our topics was Ancient Greece and included the questions: 'What made ancient Greek fighters so powerful?' and 'Was the Battle of Marathon a great victory for the ancient Greeks?' This clearly offered huge potential for cross-curricular work. Firstly, in our Design and Technology lessons we used pottery as one resource for finding out about the equipment, armour and weapons used by the ancient Greeks. We followed this up by making and decorating pots and by making our own armour. Meanwhile, we were learning about the Battle of Marathon. When the armour was finally ready, we dressed up and went into the playground to recreate the battle – as best we could! We spent some time slowly working through the stages of the battle, arranging ourselves in positions that matched what we had learned about the battle. When we were finally happy that we understood how the battle had progressed, we acted it out, marching and running around the playground, chasing the Persians back to their ships, sending Philippides on his long run back to Athens. During all this we took photographs which were later displayed in the classroom after we had added captions and text in our ICT lessons.

The final stage was to write about the battle in our Literacy lessons. During the year we had looked at various forms of poetry, including concrete and narrative poetry. I divided the class into groups, giving each of them a different stage of the battle. While the intention was that the finished poem would tell the story of the whole battle, the aim was not for each group to use a straightforward narrative but to use whatever form they thought best for their part of the story. There was much animated discussion as the children made their choices. As it turned out, the first group did choose a straight narrative form to begin the story, describing the arrival of the Persians and Philippides' unsuccessful run to Sparta to ask for help. However, the other groups made more unconventional choices. After a short verse which introduces their section, the second group used blocks of text as a way of trying to suggest troops lined up for battle. It looked very dramatic on the page. The third group made different choices again – a spiral was used to represent the turning point of the battle, the point at which the Greeks begin to win. Next, reading from the bottom of the page, words represented the path the Greeks took to chase the Persians back to the ships. The final group had to recreate Philippides' run to Marathon to tell of the miraculous victory; words stagger across the page to suggest his exhaustion (see Figure 6.1).

This work has remained with me as a vivid memory. I remember the buzz of activity, the enthusiasm in the children's voices as they played with the form on the page, their eagerness to share their work with the rest of the class. It was not just a question of putting words on a page. They understood that how they put the words on the page was as important as the words themselves; the presentation added another layer of meaning. At the end there was a real feeling of pride as the whole thing came together; they felt they had produced something original and exciting. Finally, the finished versions were displayed, alongside the armour we had made and the photographs of our re-enactment of the Battle of Marathon. Rather than the frustration I so often felt at the end of a History topic, I felt a real sense of satisfaction – we had covered the History syllabus well this time; our Literacy work had had purpose and the children had seen that Literacy skills were not just for a discrete hour in the day. There had been a sense of unity to our work. Most of all, we had enjoyed ourselves and I really believe that, through writing this poetry, there was more chance of these children remembering what happened at that battle than any other way.

Religious Studies – Stories from the News

Sometime after this, I found myself faced with a dilemma. I wanted to concentrate on teaching English but enjoyed teaching younger children and so did not want to move into secondary education. I therefore moved to an independent school as this provided a way to do this. Since then I have worked with Years 6, 7 and 8, teaching English and Religious Studies. As a primary

Philippides ran and ran from the wonderful battle to tell the good news to the king. When he stopped and heard the sound of glory and felt as if he was sprouting wings. Thud! Thud! Thud in the mud, sweating and pale and panting, Philippides sprinted until he reached the king in his noble temple and gave the good news in his croaky and broken voice. We have won! We have won! Then he fell to the feet of the king and died.

teacher I always knew what the children were learning in each subject, making it easy to find cross-curricular links. Now, with subjects taught by subject specialists from Year 4 onwards, cross-curricular work was less straightforward. However, I was in a fortunate position as my two subjects blend so well and lend themselves to cross-curricular work, especially as an important focus of our Religious Studies (RS) work was contemporary issues.

As so often happens, it was something unexpected that led to another exciting example of cross-curricular poetry writing. In 2008 I attended a special event at a local library as part of *Make a Noise in Libraries,* an annual event which aims to bring public libraries and visually-impaired people (VIP) together to improve access to books and information. As I was working with a VIP reading group as part of my PhD study, I was invited to attend this event. A local poet came to the library and read aloud a range of poems: some of his own, some well-remembered classics (Wordsworth's 'On Westminster Bridge' and 'Surprised by Joy', Keats' 'Ode on a Grecian Urn'), and some more contemporary poems, including an extract from Simon Armitage's *Killing Time* (1999), a 1,000-line poem commissioned to celebrate the Millennium. While the whole event was hugely entertaining, it was the Simon Armitage extract, beginning 'Meanwhile, somewhere in the state of Colorado...' (1999: 22–4), which really affected me. As I listened to the words, I began to realise that this was a re-working of the Columbine school massacre and the effect of hearing this extract read aloud was powerful. When I returned home, the first thing I did was to order the book.

Sometime later I decided to use the same extract with my Year 8 English class. Gradually, as I read it aloud to the children, hands slowly began to go up as a few of the children realised what the poem was really about. Afterwards these children explained their understanding of the poem, drawing in the rest of the class. By the end of the lesson, the room was filled with the stillness that you get when the children are deeply moved.

Originally I had simply intended to use the extract in our English lessons. However, the impact was so great that I felt we should do more. It so happened that I taught this class both English and RS, where, as mentioned, there is a big focus on contemporary issues. For this reason, I was constantly encouraging the children to read newspapers. I decided that we should do some cross-curricular poetry writing and that, like Simon Armitage, we should write poems based on a real event from the news.

The first stage was a session in the ICT room for the children to research news stories, searching for a stimulus for their writing. I also needed to find a story, as I always write whatever I ask the children to write. It so happened that my son's girlfriend had recently taken part in the *Lessons from Auschwitz* project, visiting the camp with other young people and a number of faith leaders including the Archbishop of Canterbury, Rowan Williams, and the Chief Rabbi, Sir Jonathan Sacks. The project aims to increase young people's knowledge and understanding of the Holocaust through a series of seminars and a one-day visit to Auschwitz. Listening to her first-hand account of this visit made a deep impression on me and so I decided to use this for my poem. Alongside the children, I sat at a computer and researched the story, using the internet to find newspaper articles and personal stories from other young people who had taken part in this project. I make no claims to be a poet – as you will see when you read the poem – but I don't think this matters. Firstly, I enjoy having a go and I find that it helps me to understand the task I have set the children. There have been a number of times when I have told them a task was easy, only to change my mind when I tried to do it myself! Furthermore, the children appreciate that I try and they enjoy the opportunity to comment on my work. The evening of the ICT session I wrote my poem to share with them in class next day:

Lessons from Auschwitz

To end the day we stood beside the tracks

which, not so long ago, brought others here

to slow starvation, misery and death.

We cupped our candles with one hand to shield

the flame and stood awhile with heads bowed down

to think of what we'd seen. Let's not forget

we'd seen it all before in books and films

but we'd been wrong to think that we had known

what to expect. Reality was worse

and now we understood why we'd been brought

to Auschwitz. It was up to us to speak

for children, men and women who'd been brought

like cattle to the slaughterhouse. We stood

beside the tracks in silent thought – and then

one boy moved to the side, all on his own,

and knelt, raised up his arms and looked to heaven.

Could prayers be heard in such a godless place?

I raised my head and, through the ghostly gloom,

a rainbow arced across the sky. A sign

of hope, a promise linking heaven and earth

that God does not abandon us in death.

Almost every detail from this poem had come from my research; the candles and the rainbow were really recorded in the articles and diary extracts I had read. I showed these to the class and modelled how I had used my notes to write the poem. I also explained where the idea for the boy kneeling to one side had come from. This had not come from my research but from real experience. In my previous school (a Catholic school) we had been on a residential trip. As we prepared to return home, we said final prayers beside the coach in the playground. At the end of this, one boy came up to me and asked if he could say a prayer of his own. I thought he meant as part of the group prayer; instead he walked a short distance from us, knelt down in the playground in full view of all the other schools preparing to leave, bowed his head and prayed silently. I found this incredibly moving. For some reason this memory had come back to me when I was working on the poem.

The children began work and, just as with the Greek poems, they were free to choose their form. Each chose a different news story, including the 'Baby P' tragedy, when a young child was killed by sustained violence from abusive adults:

The Baby P Tragedy

After nine months the punch bag is born,

Smiling like the sun on a bright day.

Looking forward to his new life

But no, what is to await him.

Cries of pain creep under and out of the room

Like water seeping out of the bath.

Kicks and punches thrown into the stomach,

And the crack of bones and the blood stained clothes,

Lie in disarray on the floor,

the flat full of rubbish and repulsive smells.

Social services come and go like sun in England

Sixty times but find nothing.

Bruises blossom like dark orchids,

A battered face, and a head which has no life left.

Once asleep but woke but now ready to fall asleep

again.

Another of our RS topics, David and Bathsheba, led us to talk about power and the misuse of power. One of the figures who came up in this part of the course was Harold Shipman, a GP in Manchester who misused his power as a doctor to prey on the elderly. One of the girls decided to use this story as the stimulus for an acrostic poem:

Murder

Hatred lingered over families

A man with an addiction to flowers gave

Random people, mostly

Old women, special attention

Life turned to the motionlessness of the dead

Diomorphine was misused

Secrets of his life were revealed

His prison bed sheets littered

In

Petals from each and every life destroyed with anguish

Men and women, mothers and fathers, brothers and sisters.

At last the final petal fell to the prison floor

Never would you think this could grow from birth so

    what is it that makes a person that kind?

I, personally, love the way these poems reflect the way the children had been inspired by the poetry they had read; for example, the final lines of the Harold Shipman poem clearly echo the last two lines of the Simon Armitage extract with the double meaning of the word 'kind'. Rather than be concerned about this, I remind the children of what Philip Pullman writes in his Acknowledgements at the end of *The Amber Spyglass*:

> I have stolen ideas from every book I have ever read. My principle in researching for a novel is 'Read like a butterfly, write like a bee', and if this story contains any honey, it is entirely because of the quality of the nectar I found in the work of better writers. (Pullman, 2000: not numbered)

I feel that using these ideas shows that the work of these writers was indeed nectar for these children, something that has enriched them as writers and as people and that will continue to nourish them. I don't believe this was simple copying; I believe it is a reflection of how fundamentally these lines had touched their readers and I hope Simon Armitage would be thrilled to see how his work had inspired young people to create something wonderful of their own.

Classics – National Poetry Day: Heroes and Heroines

Linking English and RS was straightforward for me as I taught both subjects. However, other subjects also provided rich material for cross-curricular work. The theme of National Poetry Day 2009 was *Heroes and Heroines*. Teaching at a school where the children learned Latin, this seemed a real opportunity.

I therefore spoke to the Latin teacher and found that he was planning to work on Theseus and the Minotaur and stories from the *Odyssey*. However, he knew that he would not have time to cover all the stories he'd like to. He therefore welcomed the link with English as I could work on some of these stories with the classes I taught. For my part, I was excited as our work would forge a link between subjects and show the children that their English lessons do not exist in isolation.

I decided to work on the story of 'The Sack of Winds' from the *Odyssey*. As they try to return to Ithaka, Odysseus' men have to row as there is no wind. Eventually, they come to the island of Aiolia ruled by King Aeolus, the keeper of the winds. As a gift, Aeolus ties up in a bag all the winds except the west wind which is to blow Odysseus home. Everything goes well until Odysseus falls asleep just as they are approaching Ithaka and his men open the sack, thinking it contains treasure and angry that Odysseus has not shared it with them. At once the winds escape; a great storm whips up and the ship, so close to home, is blown off course and back to Aiolia.

I read this story with my Year 7 class and then we discussed how we might write poetry about the story. We looked at some acrostic poems about Medusa and some of the children chose this as the form for their poem, as in the example below:

> **S**ea water as still as a millpond
>
> **A**ll the winds in a sack
>
> **C**oming upon that island was fate
>
> **K**ing Aeolus gave them that sack, which carried him all the way home
>
> **O**dysseus saw his home
>
> **F**arms, friends and family so close to him
>
> **W**ith relief came tiredness
>
> **I**diotic sailors, greedy for gold, opened the sack
>
> **N**ow the wind and smoke were out of the bag
>
> **D**rowning waves everywhere
>
> **S**tormy weather, as bad as it gets.

However, some of the children decided they would rather use a freer form and told the story their own way:

> The sea, calm, smooth, peaceful
>
> Our ship gliding, flowing, skating over it
>
> We have a sack of winds

Given to us by the king – we were told not to open it.

Sailing through the water for nine days and nights

Minute by minute getting closer to Ithaka

Waiting patiently for the moment to glimpse her.

There, behind that cloud, there she is.

The sea, clear, still, unmoving

Our ship, gaining, waiting, hopeful.

This journey is worth it.

I'm within 100 metres of her, savouring every moment

My stupid, idiotic crew open the bag.

With a blinding light and deafening crack

The skies open and the sea grows angry, frightening, furious

Our ship, thrown side to side and battled against.

We are afraid, being tossed to and fro,

Climbing and falling each steep wave.

It is true; the sea wants to punish us

We are plunging deep into the waves below the surface

Deeper and deeper, away from the ones we love.

The sea, satisfied, triumphant, glorious

Our ship, drowned, broken, lost.

Deciding to link with the Latin teacher had another advantage. He was so interested in what we were doing that, on National Poetry Day, he organised for his form to go up to people all around the school and offer to read them a poem. Poetry was all around in a vibrant way instigated by a teacher outside of the English department. For that day, that Latin teacher was certainly my hero!

Conclusions

Attending the *Literacy: What Works?* conference was a key moment in my development as an English teacher. As someone who was inexperienced at the time, my teaching was dominated by the National Literacy Strategy. The conference inspired me to break free from these constraints and approach my teaching in a more open, creative way, and cross-curricular work was an important part of this. However, this was no fad. The continued importance of cross-curricular work was reflected in the final report of the *Independent Review of the Primary Curriculum* (DCSF, 2009) which explicitly refers to the importance of cross-curricular work as a way of strengthening learning:

> Our primary schools also show that high standards are best secured when essential knowledge and skills are learned both through direct, high-quality subject teaching and also through this content being applied and used in cross-curricular studies. (p. 2)

These proposed changes to the primary curriculum, though not subsequently implemented by the new UK government, were seen as a move away from fixed subjects to broad areas of learning. Organising the curriculum in this way looks for a blending of high quality subject-specific teaching and equally challenging cross-curricular studies. However, while cross-curricular work can be advocated as a way of strengthening learning, more integrated learning can also be a strategy for saving curriculum time. Furthermore, cross-curricular work is not the exclusive domain of primary schools. The secondary curriculum also contains cross-curricular dimensions and the NC English programme of study at Key Stage 3 states that pupils should have opportunities to develop skills in speaking, listening, reading and writing through work that makes links with other subjects.

I was fortunate to attend *Poetry Live for Haiti* in January 2010, an event organised by the Poet Laureate Carol Ann Duffy to raise funds for the Haiti Earthquake Appeal. The event was introduced by the then UK Prime Minister Gordon Brown who said that:

> [P]oetry does what ordinary words can never by themselves achieve. Instead of narrowing our view of the world, poetry broadens and deepens our understanding, recognises the diversity and richness of our experience, and where power can be blind to human needs, poetry can cleanse and inspire. (http://www.number10.gov.uk/Page22321)

In some ways, the whole *Poetry Live for Haiti* event embodied the idea of cross-curricular poetry. For example, three of the poets read poems they had written as a response to a specific event – Elaine Feinstein's 'Port au Prince', Gillian Clarke's 'Lament' and Roger McGough's 'They Came Out Singing'. However, in my opinion, the event also reflected the cross-curricular dimensions of the NC. One of these dimensions – 'the global dimension and sustainable development' – includes the question, 'How can I become an active global citizen?', while another of the dimensions – 'creativity and critical thinking'– poses the question, 'Why are cultural experiences relevant to me and how can I get involved as a spectator, participant or creator?' The poets that day were surely using this cultural event as a way of being involved as active global citizens.

Linking literacy teaching to other curriculum areas has a number of advantages. When the work was linked to another subject, I always felt that I understood why we were producing a particular piece of writing and I believe that the children must also have felt that the writing was purposeful. We always had lots to write about, as the content came from something that had been studied; this is always an advantage for children who find it difficult to think of ideas. Furthermore, cross-curricular work breaks down the compartmentalisation of the curriculum and shows that the skills taught in English lessons do not just belong in a neat box.

Over the years, I have used cross-curricular work as the stimulus for all sorts of writing: reports on life in Victorian times; explanations of the water cycle; persuasive writing about healthy eating. However, the most memorable examples all came from poetry writing. There is no doubt that cross-curricular poetry seems to steer the children away from the glib, rhyming poetry they so often turn to. I believe this is because they automatically realise, with no steering from me, that what they want to write cannot be communicated effectively through rhyming poetry. While it is true that the examples I have given use a number of forms (shape poems, acrostics, narrative poems), the form has always been selected as most appropriate to the meaning. Meaning always comes first.

Furthermore, I believe that writing cross-curricular poetry helps children to see that poetry is not obscure. They see what inspires poets. Classical mythology, such as the story of Odysseus, may have inspired classic poets like Tennyson in his poem 'Ulysses', but it continues to inspire contemporary poets, as we see in Carol Ann Duffy's collection *The World's Wife* (1999). The children and I took our inspiration from the same source as other poets. Similarly, to mark the deaths of Henry Allingham and Harry Patch, two of the last surviving Britons to fight in the First World War, Carol Ann Duffy wrote a poem entitled 'Last Post' (http://www.guardian.co.uk/uk/2009/jul/31/carol-ann-duffy-last-post). This poem was inspired by a past war; this is exactly what we were doing in writing about the Battle of Marathon. Just as Simon Armitage was inspired by a particular news story, so were we. In this way, cross-curricular work such as that described here can provide important continuities with the real world of poetry outside the classroom walls.

SOMETHING TO THINK ABOUT

Cross-curricular teaching is based on the assumption that English underpins and supports all aspects of the curriculum. However, teachers can be protective of their subject and prefer subjects to be taught discretely. How do you and your colleagues view the relationship between English and other curriculum subjects?

SOMETHING TO READ

The Works 2: Poems on Every Subject and for Every Occasion, compiled by Brian Moses and Pie Corbett (2002) is an anthology of poems relating to all areas of the curriculum and therefore a very useful resource for any cross-curricular poetry work.

SOMETHING TO DO

Discuss with colleagues the profile of poetry in your school's planning. Perhaps carry out an audit of cross-curricular opportunities. Can you find any specific references to poetry being used to support other curriculum areas? Think about some ways you could develop this within your own practice and school.

References

Armitage, S. (1999) *Killing Time*. London: Faber & Faber.

Department for Children, Schools and Families (DCSF) (2009) *Independent Review of the Primary Curriculum: Final Report* [The Rose Review]. London: DCSF.

Duffy, C.A. (1999) *The World's Wife*. London: Picador.

Moses, B. & Corbett, P. (2002) *The Works 2: Poems on Every Subject and for Every Occasion*. 3rd edn. London: Macmillan.

Palmer, S. & Corbett, P. (2003) *Literacy: What Works?* Cheltenham: Nelson Thorne.

Pullman, P. (2000) *The Amber Spyglass*. London: Scholastic.

Websites

http://www.number10.gov.uk/Page22321

http://www.guardian.co.uk/uk/2009/jul/31/carol-ann-duffy-last-post

Chapter 7

Teaching Poetry to Teenagers

Lionel Warner

CHAPTER OVERVIEW

This chapter considers key issues involved in teaching poetry to teenagers and provides examples of good classroom practice, focusing on the lower secondary school or KS3 phase. It is organised around three areas of enquiry: progression from KS2 and towards KS4 (14–16 years), the integration of reading and writing, and the cross-curricular dimension in poetry within a subject-based secondary curriculum. The importance of integrating form and content in approaches to poetry with this age-group is emphasised throughout.

I have a pet interview question which goes something like this:

> I was in a school yesterday where the teacher told me that her Year 9 class groan when you mention poetry; what can you as an English teacher do to overcome the groan factor?

The question is a valuable one, partly because it is true to experience, and partly because it evokes a valuable range of ideas from interviewees on ways of promoting enjoyment in the classroom. The recommendation of a focus on enjoyment is long-standing. For example, Strong (1961) laments widespread British indifference to poetry, says schools are to blame, and recommends that teachers of poetry 'put enjoyment first, second, third and fourth' (p. 16). More recently, Snapper (2009) feels that the increased separation between the oral and the literary tradition as children move though secondary school, and an increased emphasis on writing examination essays, contribute to a sense of alienation from poetry which can persist into higher education and beyond. It seems also to be the case now that though much poetry is taught in schools, less poetry is studied at degree level by prospective English teachers (Stevens, 2007).

The current climate in some secondary schools may not readily foster the free enjoyment of poetry and may pose particular problems for poetry teachers. A beginning English teacher recently told me that she is not alone in her department in finding that although the unit of work on poetry in Year 8 (ages 12–13) is enjoyable and stimulating, it is difficult to 'level' (i.e. assess) the pupils at the end of the unit because the levelling instrument for reading is a Point-Example-Explanation (PEE) essay, and this does not seem to work so well for poetry. A teacher in another school tells me about the sudden appearance of the 'butterfly manager' in the classroom, keeping staff on their eternally pre-Ofsted inspection toes, sitting down next to a pupil and demanding to know what *the* lesson objective is (my emphasis) – note the singular here, which would have caused problems for me and my pupils in all the poetry lessons I taught. We perhaps need to write up 'enjoyment' as the lesson objective more often. The challenge is to combat its erosion.

The problem may be that in our culture and society, and therefore in our classrooms, we put poetry on a pedestal. We make it too rarefied and mystical, demanding in its presence a hushed reverence as if in art gallery or church. Some say this tendency was caused by the advent of New Criticism in the early twentieth century. Or perhaps we don't treat poetry as special enough. Poetry is sometimes treated in our classrooms as collections of devices to be logged, a technical rather than an enjoyable or aesthetic experience.

If there is not a unitary problem with poetry there are certainly some challenges that teaching it presents and which emerge with particular force when teaching teenagers during the early years of secondary school. In discussing the teaching of poetry at KS3 I have three areas of enquiry: progression; reading and writing; and the cross-curricular dimension. When I was discussing this chapter with a school colleague she defended her department by saying 'maybe we buck the trend but we are all English teachers who enjoy teaching poetry' and went on to maintain that their pupils enjoy poetry too. I want on balance to argue that they don't buck the trend, they are the trend.

Some of the challenges can be illustrated by an account of three incidents in my recent professional experience.

I am observing a Year 6 teacher who has on the screen R.L. Stevenson's 'From a Railway Carriage' in an attractive software page. The poem is being used as a starter and the pupils have to identify the similes. There are two: 'like troops in a battle' and 'as thick as driving rain'. There is no attempt to address or respond to the more striking technical feature of this poem, its triplet-rhythm evoking the jaunty movement of the train. I suggest in my debrief that the teacher has missed an opportunity to give an overview of the poem to complement the close, detailed reading. I suggest two overview ideas: it would have been both fun and illuminating to rearrange the desks and attempt some kind of choric reading with the whole class seated as if in the train; and, bearing in mind the attractive children's book graphics on the screen and the imagery in Stevenson's poem such as 'a mill' and 'a cart runaway in the road', it would have been stimulating to ask the class what suggests that the poem might have been written a long time ago.

I then come across this on an exam board's website, in a report on a General Certificate of Secondary Education (GCSE) examination for KS4 students:

> In their responses to poetry it was felt that too many candidates still fail to provide an overview of the poems they are comparing or discussing. Many, after an introductory explanation of what they are intending to do, spend an often very lengthy second paragraph identifying, in considerable detail, rhyme schemes, punctuation, enjambment and oxymorons, usually without any comment on the effect of such devices or close reference to the poems. The identification of devices becomes a substitute for a response to what the poets are communicating and how they are using the language to communicate with the reader. This 'how' goes beyond an arid listing of which devices are being used. Some candidates found it difficult to support and illustrate the rather surprising claim that the use of punctuation 'vividly conveyed personal feelings'. (OCR, 2007: 8)

I do not accuse all KS2 teachers of treating poetry in that reductive way, nor all KS4 teachers, but there is an issue here of teaching and progression.

I then arrive in the English staff room of a nearby comprehensive secondary school; I am there to observe a poetry lesson and to talk to some of the staff. As I enter the room an animated voice asks if everyone has read a recent email. It is from a colleague forwarding remarks made in a *Guardian* (2010) newspaper article by a former Poet Laureate about the teaching or rather the mis-teaching of poetry in secondary school. Teachers are accused of a number of sins: underestimating pupils' intelligence; stifling their creativity; exhorting pupils to do no more than add up the similes and spot the alliteration; lacking confidence; and passing on their anxieties about poetry to their pupils. The animated voice is angry.

I think there is a more optimistic view of the teaching of poetry in KS3 than the above might suggest. It is, of course, not easy. A poem may be brief, but it rarely yields up what it has to offer at a first, brisk reading. Examiners as well as teachers acknowledge a high level of demand: 'Poetry is literary language at its most intense' (CIE, 2008: 10). There are many poems which themselves attempt to address the paradoxical mystery and yet directness of poetry. Archibald MacLeish's 'Ars Poetica' famously ends with the vatic: 'A poem should not mean/But be'. Sue Dymoke's poem 'How Does a Poem Mean?' addresses a similar point. Steve Horsfall's 'The Definition of Poetry' also makes it sound both easy and difficult, ending 'you know it when you hear it'. And Billy Collins' 'Introduction to Poetry' says that we should be able to 'take a poem/and hold it up to the light', but the trouble is that we 'begin beating it with a hose/to find out what it really means'. Are poems about poetry helpful for KS3 pupils? I'm never sure. Is 'To Autumn' ('thou hast thy music too') qualitatively different in this respect from Keats' other great Odes, or are they all about art? I remember a number of deep discussions about this when I was in my own teens. We are here approaching a post-structuralist view that all texts are about texts. Does that way madness lie for young teenagers? Should poems be real and relevant? Knowing their pupils, these are important question for KS3 English teachers to address.

My favourite illustration of the intense, condensed power of poetry is the last line of one of my favourite poems, 'Love III', by George Herbert: 'So I did sit and eat.' It is in effect a sentence, of six tiny words, with short vowels and definite dental consonants: morphologically and syntactically as simple as it gets. Semantically too, the line reflects an unremarkable everyday action. But it is also the quiet climax of a parable of uncertainty and hesitancy. The speaker's final acceptance is underscored by the line's regular iambic metre, perfectly natural to speech and also emphasising the three key semantic words. And of course the act of eating in the context of this poem and writer has symbolic, sacramental overtones. We want to help teenage pupils towards these perceptions and under-standings. English teachers are only too aware that the seeds planted in their KS3 classes grow to fruition well after the end of unit assessment and the sum-mative level. We must also remember that there is a background radiation of parental and cultural attitudes to poetry in long-term operation (Lambirth, 2007).

In the pre-NLS days my approach to teaching poetry in what is now called KS3 was often 'the occasional treat'. But the occasions were frequent, and the treat was genuine. I was trained in a tradition that combined poetry study with other sources in packages called 'themes'. So for example, half a term's work in English might be labelled 'homelessness' or 'outcasts', and as part of this the class would read and discuss poems such as Dylan Thomas' 'Hunchback in the Park'. The apparent revolution of the NLS was to map and plan progression, so as to ratchet up the demands of the various areas of English. The aim of the map/plan was to 'underwrite the ratchet' (Hackman, 2001). The problem, never mind the essentially recursive nature of English, rapidly became how to negotiate the huge complexity of the curriculum thus construed. There were two immediate responses, both of which affected poetry: first the evolution of key objectives, which did not foreground poetry, and second the use of poetry (short poems, or extracts from longer ones) in lesson starters to focus attention on particularities, such as metaphor or allit-eration, or even spelling. Poetry became a kind of brain gym. It seems to me now at least arguable that 'treat', 'theme' and 'ratchet' are not very different from each other, and are similar in two senses. They are potentially equally plausible as useful approaches to keeping poetry alive in English. As always, it depends how it's done. And they actually blend or morph into each other, as practice shows.

What else? Do we as English teachers pay enough attention to the sound of poetry? Gordon (2004) thinks not. My view is that for every poem that benefits from being *heard* in the classroom there is another one that benefits from being closely *read*. Do pupils want strong meanings, or do they enjoy investigating the formal features of words on the page? Peskin (2007) thinks the latter, including those who claim at first not to like poetry. Can teachers of KS3 pupils begin to get them to see the intimate links between form and content in poetry? Central curriculum guidance may have been less than helpful to teachers in this respect (Wilson, 2005), yet it is my contention that they are nevertheless making it happen.

So, as in all teaching, we want to make it easier for our pupils, and also more difficult.

Progression Between Key Stages

KS2 to KS3

It is to be hoped and indeed planned that pupils during the course of KS3 develop a sense of the marriage of form and content in poetry. This is an important dimension when we consider progression.

I used to worry about haiku. Other Year 7 (ages 11–12) teachers used to tell me they were having enjoyable lessons on haiku. In my Year 7 class I used to find that although they all claimed they had 'done it before' in primary school many of the class did not know the 5-7-5 syllable count and some were not able to count the syllables accurately. More importantly, they needed guidance on the point or purpose a haiku might serve. Yes it is a snapshot, so pupils should be able in a few words to evoke something seen. Traditionally a haiku also makes reference to the season, so both its form and content evoke a sense of transience. Year 7 pupils can grasp this idea; when they write haiku they should try to capture something before it escapes.

Another progression issue I used to worry about concerned limericks, partly because the only limericks that spring to my mind are wholly inappropriate for classroom use, but also and more importantly because of the fear of mere repetition of primary level work. But I think our pupils may be in safe hands. I sat in recently on a Year 7 lesson taught by a beginning teacher in which the agenda explicitly built on and extended prior knowledge. The teacher established that her pupils knew about the rhyme scheme and humorous effect of a limerick; in their class reading she gave them a taste of the history of the form and the range of its effects, including the whimsical Edward Lear as well as smart-alec limericks about relativity. When they wrote they were challenged to write an 'anti-limerick', a task embodying an understanding of form and content, and produced some satisfyingly surreal poems such as this:

There once was a man from Dover

Whose favourite food was clover

He jumped in his car

And sped to the bar

And now his favourite food is beer.

Another progression route I have found helpful in this area is the classroom study of the cinquain. This kind of poem has a strict form, five lines with a 2-4-6-8-2 syllable count, and tends as a result to build to a climax at the end of the fourth line. I used to put it to my pupils that they should aim for a mini-cliffhanger. So, for example, these from Year 7 pupils:

Look! My

Green marble is

Rolling towards the edge

Of the shiny grey desk top, and

Falls off!

Let's see.

I wonder if

There are any biscuits

Left. Lift the lid off and find out.

All gone.

For examples of cinquains and other poetic forms appropriate for this stage of transition from primary school to KS3 a helpful source is Gerard Benson's anthology *This Poem Doesn't Rhyme* (1990).

Similarly the 'telephone poem' can develop pupils' sense of form and content. It is a very personal form since you take your own phone number, which gives you the number of syllables (or words, if that makes it easier) per line, and zero equals a line space. The challenge is then to make the poem personal to you, or, to add an extra element of challenge, make the poem someone calling you.

KS3 to KS4

Looking forward to progression to KS4, the choice of poem for Year 9s (ages 13–14) to read is key. Seamus Heaney's 'The Early Purges' has potential: the poem is provocative as well as stylistically interesting, and Heaney is often studied in KS4. Yandell (2003) recalls KS3 use of the poem as a starter activity. Working first with words and phrases taken from the poem, before reading the poem itself, was found to be particularly successful. If you choose the words well you can highlight Heaney's tough sensuousness, and the experience and feelings of the boy, and then come to an overview of the poem, an effective focus for which is the question of whether the last line is ironic: '... on well-run farms pests have to be kept down'.

The poem is not only provocative but distressing. I use an exercise with PGCE trainee teachers which involves a paired parents' evening improvisation. Each 'parent' of the pair is briefed to raise two concerns about the classroom use of this poem: first, that the Year 9 pupil came home distressed about the graphic depiction of drowning kittens, and second that the poem contains bad language. The 'teacher' of course has to some extent at least to defend the poem and its use. The exercise is useful for trainees in highlighting some aspects of parents' evening protocol, but it also raises issues about poetry in the classroom. As pupils get older the literature they study will pose uncomfortable questions and provoke deep emotions, and English teachers must be able to defend challenging material. This will sometimes involve taboo language, and they need to be able to confront this issue too. The kittens are not only called 'shits' by Dan Taggart in the poem, but the word also refers to the way they are treated, thrown on the 'dunghill'. Year 9 pupils are fully capable of understanding the effect of these word choices.

English teachers should perhaps beware of thinking that texts somehow belong with certain age groups or key stages, though of course it is helpful to organise a departmental or national curriculum by doing so. Many a so-called Advanced Level (A-level) novel has been successfully taught at GCSE, for example. It is instructive, then, to consider the ways in which Shakespeare's Sonnet 18 and Carol Ann Duffy's 'Valentine' have both been successfully used in KS3.

I undertook some observation of teaching and discussion of poetry teaching around the time of Valentine's Day. A Year 8 top set had clearly had a recent rich poetry diet. They had studied Tennyson's 'The Lady of Shallot'. They knew about pathetic fallacy; if not the term then certainly the idea that natural images might be used to represent human feelings. The pupils were first given the line from Sonnet 18, 'Shall I compare thee to a summer's day?' and were asked in pairs to think about:

- who might be asking this question?
- who might be asked the question?
- why you might compare someone to a summer's day?

As they were talking about this, a montage of photos depicting a summer's day came up on the screen, including ice cream, a crowded beach, a downpour and other pictures both positive and negative. The teacher's questions provoked a variety of ideas about why someone would want to make this comparison. Then she distributed copies of Shakespeare's sonnet and read it aloud to the class. The pupils now had to find ways in which the poet was making the comparison. Many in their discussion began by seeing conventional comparisons, but soon began to see that the poet refers to a summer's day's shortcomings and that therefore the addressee is superior, an altogether better compliment. Few got as far as the 'so long lives this' conclusion of the poem, but interestingly a group of girls did begin to interpret the everlastingness of the final lines in the light of their current reading, and asked 'Do you think he's a vampire, Miss?'. The pupils were then led to compose their own 'Shall I compare thee' poem for Valentine's Day. Work was animated and engaged. For example, boys near me began: 'Shall I compare you to a BMW? You are more classy and ...'

In another school a Year 9 bottom set had clearly undergone a similarly rich and creative process. They had read Duffy's 'Valentine', and had produced a wall display of their own poetry for Valentine's Day in response, of which pupils and teachers were justifiably proud. They had clearly grasped the challenge to the conventional and the sense of developed metaphor in the original poem. For example, a favourite poem of mine on display in the classroom began 'I give you a radiator', and went on to suggest that its warmth might not always be turned on. Another poem read:

The Paper

Not a red rose or a satin heart

I give you a pile of paper

We can make it into anything

We can fly around.

If our love's rubbish

We can start again.

These pupils to my mind clearly know in some sense all about the marriage of form and content.

Duffy's 'Valentine' has been a KS4 GCSE staple for some years. Shakespeare's sonnets continue to be set for A-level. Yet KS3 pupils are making sense of both. Here, in the sensitive hands of teachers who know their pupils, is the way forward for progression into KS4.

Poetry Reading and Poetry Writing

The above instances of teaching demanding poems serve not only as examples of preparing pupils for poetry at KS4 but also as examples of integrating the reading and the writing of poetry; writing seen sometimes as a starter or 'way into' the poem, and sometimes as a product and end result. Students in my experience are often pleased to discover that they have written a poem and that their poem has an honourable pedigree. This process of integration is commonplace and principled. Kroll and Evans (2006) suggest that integrating the reading and writing of poetry can combat the boredom and indifference felt by pupils when faced with poetry. Linaberger (2004), similarly, argues that the integration of writing and reading poetry helps to constitute for teachers a method of overcoming the feeling of threat posed by poetry.

At a different school in the same borough as those above, I observed another low ability Year 8 set, who had studied 'The Lady of Shallot' and enjoyed its romance and drama. This lesson was another enthusiastic interlinking of reading and writing poetry. The teacher began by asking the pupils to brainstorm 'poet': what sort of person, personality and so on. The responses were revealing: 'someone who wears frilly collars', 'well mannered and kind – their poems come from the heart', 'emotional', 'wise', 'lonely … in his own world', 'posh – not a chav'. As a corrective to this remarkable persistence of the Romantic image, the class were played a video of Benjamin Zephaniah performing 'Talking Turkeys'. They then discussed differences between their prior image of a poet and this one. The teacher asked them to think of 'things that matter to you', serious or light-hearted, and to perform a rap on one of these subjects. All the pupils, in a far from top set, devised something in the time, and again showed implicit understanding of a relationship between form and content: the rhythmical nature of the rap and the sense of 'things that matter'. One was a tribute to the pupil's family, which began:

> My family mean the world to me, I don't know where to start.
>
> If anything did happen it would deffo break my heart.

The influence of the original Zephaniah poem is evident not just in the rhyme but also the regular rhythm and idiomatic language. Another pupil's poem asked us to be kind to those with red hair and contained the vivid line: 'fire burning on the ginger's head'.

A last word here about the impact of technology. Many excellent websites support the reading and enjoyment of poetry for all ages and it would be invidious to highlight just a few of them. Examples abound of the use of new technology in poetry teaching. For instance, Baines (2001) offers an interesting project for those who have yet to explore the possibilities of new technology in his 'hometown poems'. Dymoke (2009b) explores drafting and composing on screen, the use of hypertext and wikis, and new forms such as text message poetry. Beavis (2008) cites computer games being used to teach poetic writing as well as reading. Classroom technology offers the teacher expanded means of engaging diverse classes, whether we think of differences in ethnicity, language background or learning style (Vincent, 2005).

Beach and O'Brien (2005) point out two particular effects of the rich multi-modal intertextuality which many pupils are used to. The first is the erosion of the distinction between consuming and producing, between reading and writing. A good example of this is *YouTube* interpretations of 'From a Railway Carriage'. The second is the increase in shared practices. As I write I have recently visited the 'Romantics' exhibition at Tate Britain, which features the iconic 'Death of Chatterton' by Henry Wallis, a picture embodying the isolation of the artist. The cultural view of poetry in particular as something both produced and consumed in solitude is persistent, as the Year 8s above reminded us, and may help to account for difficulties in the poetry classroom. New technology, however, leads to more social activity.

Poetry and Other Subjects

Music teachers tell me they sometimes use poems in their classrooms which have a strong sound or otherwise sensuous content for which pupils can make a soundscape with musical instruments. See, for example, the recommended treatment of Tennyson's 'The Kraken' in *When Words Sing* (BCMG, 2008). The opening of Noyes' 'The Highwayman' (1906) also contains very obvious references to sound such as the wind in the 'gusty' trees, clattering on cobbles as the horseman enters the inn yard, and the tune he whistles to Bess, the landlord's daughter. There are also more subtle opportunities for interpretation, such as the 'twinkle' of his rapier and pistol, and Bess' thoughts of love as she plaits her hair. It is then worth looking at the last two stanzas of the poem to see how these elements are reprised. As another example, 'Sound count down' by Robert Hull (2003), a poem about the sounds someone can hear while waiting for the bathroom to be free, is an amusing opportunity for percussion interpretation.

Geography also seems to be a surprisingly poetic field (if you'll pardon the pun):

> ... most poetry is imbued with explicit and vivid references to physical and human phenomena over space, and is thus a source of information that may help illustrate a variety of geographic concepts. (Donaldson, 2001: 24)

Matthewman and Morgan (2006) see geographical possibilities in Les Murray's poem 'Pigs', though I'm not sure its language is appropriate for KS3. A selection of poetry from an anthology prescribed for examination once included Auden's poem 'In Praise of Limestone'. Quite how this poem, which is certainly difficult and possibly inappropriate, made the list remains a mystery and was probably a mistake, and I later discovered in talking to the principal examiner that questions would not be set on it. However, members of my department at the time asked me to suggest how it might be taught. This led to one of my earliest attempts at action research, in which I devised three different teaching approaches to the poem and asked students to evaluate them. One approach was heavily didactic (the kind of teaching of poetry routinely criticised), and another involved what was intended to be sensitive questioning (my favoured approach at the time, and probably now). The third featured treatment of the same subject matter in a completely different genre, that is to say, beginning with a geography film about limestone pavements and drawing some comparisons. (For the record, evaluation results suggested didacticism was least effective).

I have often thought the third approach might pay dividends with classes. There are vivid scientific films about the nature and growth of fungi which could effectively follow a reading of Plath's 'Mushrooms', for example, in order to throw into relief both her pictorial descriptions, shared by the film, and her mounting sense of unease, which may or may not be shared by pupils. It is a highly engaging lesson first to give a Year 8 or 9 class the text of this poem without its title, asking them to make suggestions. It is important to read and perform the poem, bringing out the distinctive dum-di-di-dum-di rhythmic signature of many of the lines, such as: 'Nobody sees us', 'Earless and eyeless' or 'Nudgers and shovers'. Here form conveys the quietly threatening meaning.

Most teachers I have talked to say that it is in history they are most likely to use poetry in their lessons, in particular in the KS3 study of the First World War. In part this seems to me to add to the phenomenon. What is World War I known for? Trenches, gas, no man's land, poets. In another respect the poetry provides valuable sources, both of fact and opinion: if you want a picture of rats or lice, where better to go then the poetry of Isaac Rosenberg; if you want a source that conveys a strong view about war and patriotism, where better to go than Wilfred Owen's 'Dulce et Decorum Est'?

The relationship between history and poetry is particularly interesting in the case of World War I. It may seem hard to maintain a focus on the poetry when the poems are seen as historical documents, although all the teachers I have spoken to, teachers of both history and English, adopt something very like Owen's view that the poetry is in the pity and that the emotional power of the poetry is inescapable. Nevertheless a tendency develops in pupils to regard the testimony of the poems as an ultimate truth, because the poets were 'there', despite their history teachers' insistence that they evaluate sources. This leads to the persistence, as Stephen (1996) argues, of certain myths. For example the idea that the ordinary British soldier felt more kinship with the ordinary Germans in the nearby trenches (witness the Christmas Day football and gifts) than with his own remote and exploitative senior officers is, in his view, misguided.

The revised secondary National Curriculum has seven 'cross-curriculum dimensions' (QCDA, n.d.) and it would be the task of another chapter to suggest poems to illuminate them all. The Poetry Society, however, is excited at this challenge 'not to dilute poetry [but] to encourage poetic forms of understanding in all aspects of learning and life' (Colley and Dahouk, 2010: 19). Stevens (2005), for example, describes the use of Craig Raine's poem 'A Martian Sends a Postcard Home' to teach Citizenship in Year 8, reinforcing my view that Citizenship is best taught though English anyway. Archer (2007) argues that symbolic objects are powerful in opening school students' awareness across a range of topics, including globalisation. Poems are symbolic objects, as well as treatments of symbolic objects (Thomas Hardy's 'The Darkling Thrush', mushrooms, the west wind, apple picking) even if the meaning of the symbolism is various and contested. Perhaps English teachers might be consulted more by their colleagues about possibilities for poetry across the curriculum.

Conclusion

So what do I think? I think that, despite reductive dangers, poems are rich historical sources. I think that there is no more spiritual element in the secondary school curriculum than English in general and poetry in particular. I think that the intimate connection between form and content can be understood by pupils of KS3 age although there is a long way to go. I think that poetry is truly interdisciplinary in the sense that reading appropriate poems can help pupils to understand some of the links between topics and ideas which the secondary school curriculum still tends to separate. I agree with Medway (2010) that there is a cognitive as well as an emotional and aesthetic aspect to poetry which makes it all the more rich and valuable. As I said earlier, important seeds are being planted at this stage of a child's school career. And enjoyment, as the above examples from current practice indicate, is always key. The Poetry Society (2010, title page) is right to insist:

> … unless literacy starts with goosebumps, laughter, or contemplative silence, none of us would bother to read anything but bills, instructions and road signs. When teaching the reading of poetry the guide words should be: immersion, leisure, enjoyment, fun.

SOMETHING TO THINK ABOUT

Perhaps it helps not to say 'today we are doing poetry' at all. Perhaps in our planning we should put the reading and writing of poetry in a continuum of other forms and modes, still highlighting the various intertwined relationships between form and meaning, but without privileging the term 'poetry'. This is not a counsel of pedagogical cowardice, but both a rational response to technological change and also a principled desire for pupils to make their own meanings, as both consumers and producers.

SOMETHING TO READ

Have a look at the 'Poetry Trail Key Stage 3' on the Birmingham Botanical Gardens site (http://www.birminghambotanicalgardens.org.uk/images/stories/pdf/poetry_trail_ks3.pdf) – and then go and visit it.

SOMETHING TO DO

- Research the lyrics of pop songs; find some that make reasonable sense on the page and that relate to music your pupils might have heard of. Song lyrics are good to engage pupils' initial interest, to expand their ideas of what counts as poetry, and they introduce a notion of multi-modality. When you have talked about the words on the page or screen, play the song and discuss what the music adds.
- Write your own haiku/cinquain/ottava rima stanza/sonnet in class *at the same time as your pupils are doing so*, and share the results. Your pupils will love being critics of your writing and you will realise how hard the task is you have set them.

References

Archer, A. (2007) '"No Goats in the Mother City": using Symbolic Objects to Help Students Talk about Diversity and Change', *English in Education*, 41(1): 7–20.

Baines, L. (2001) 'Out of the Box', *Voices from the Middle*, 9(1): 12–20, available at: http://www.lawrencebaines.com/outofthebox.pdf (accessed 22 August 2010).

BCMG (Birmingham Contemporary Music Group) (2008) 'When Words Sing', available at: http://www.bcmg.org.uk/mmsys/modules/edit/file_send.php?id=1409 (accessed 7 September 2010).

Beach, R. & O'Brien, D. (2005) 'Playing Texts Against Each Other in the Multimodal English Classroom', *English in Education*, 39(2): 44–59.

Beavis, C. (2008) 'Paying Attention to Texts: Literacy, Culture and Curriculum', *English in Australia*, 43(1): 23–31.

Benson, G. (ed.) (1990) *This Poem Doesn't Rhyme*. London: Viking.

CIE (University of Cambridge International Examinations) (2008) IGCSE English Literature Paper 1 Mark Scheme: 0486_w08_ms_1.pdf, available at: http://www.cie.org.uk/qualifications/academic/middlesec/igcse/subject?assdef_id=853 (accessed 7 April 2010).

Collins, B. 'Introduction to Poetry', available at: http://www.poetryfoundation.org/archive/poem.html?id=176056 (accessed 7 April 2010).

Colley, B. & Dahouk, A. (2010) 'Exploring Experience: A Sea-change in Poetry Provision', *NATE Classroom*, 10: 19–21.

Donaldson, D. (2001) 'Teaching Geography's Four Traditions with Poetry', *Journal of Geography*, 100(1): 24–31.

Dymoke, S. (2009a) 'How Does a Poem Mean?', *English in Education*, 42(2): 117.

Dymoke, S. (2009b) 'Drafting, Sharing, Hearing, Seeing – Teaching Poetry with ICT', *English Drama Media*, 13: 13–20.

Gordon, J. (2004) 'Verbal Energy: Attending to Poetry', *English in Education*, 38(1): 92–103.

The Guardian (2010) 'Too much Rap, Not Enough Proper Poetry, Says Former Laureate', http://www.guardian.co.uk/education/2010/jan/07/poetry-teaching-andrew-motion (accessed 7 April 2010).

Hackman, S. (2001) Conference presentation on 'Literacy' at *Literacy in Transition*, University of Reading School of Education.

Horsfall, S. (2005) *The Definition of Poetry*, available at: http://www.oupoets.org.uk/MainPages/03-Poetry/Openings22.pdf (p. 27) (accessed 7 April 2010).

Hull, R. (2003) 'Sound Count Down', in *Don't Panic! 100 Poems to Save Your Life* chosen by F. Waters. London: Macmillan. p. 44.

Kroll, J. & Evans, S. (2006) 'Metaphor Delivers: An Integrated Approach to Teaching and Writing Poetry', available at: http://www.aate.org.au/files/documents/Kroll%20&%20Evans%2041_2%20text.pdf (accessed 22 January 2010).

Lambirth, A. (2007) 'Poetry Under Control: Social Reproduction Strategies and Children's Literature', *English in Education*, 41(3): 94–107.

Linaberger, M. (2004) 'Poetry Top 10: A Foolproof Formula for Teaching Poetry', *The Reading Teacher*, 58(4): 366–72.

Macleish, A. (1926) 'Ars Poetica', available at: http://transcriptions.english.ucsb.edu/archive/courses/liu/english25/materials/macleish.html (accessed 7 April 2010).

Matthewman, S. & Morgan, J. (2006) 'English and Geography: Common Ground? From *Planet Earth* to *Pigs*', *Changing English*, 13(3): 259–72.

Medway, P. (2010) 'English and Enlightenment', *Changing English*, 17(1): 3–12.

Noyes, A. (1906) 'The Highwayman', available, for example, at: http://www.love-poems.me.uk/noyes_the_highwayman.htm (accessed 7 April 2010).

OCR (Oxford Cambridge and RSA Examinations) (2007) 'GCSE English Literature, Report on the Units, January 2007', available at: http://www.ocr.org.uk/download/rep_07/ocr_19136_rep_07_1_gcse_jan.pdf (accessed 24 February 2010).

Peskin, J. (2007) 'The Genre of Poetry: Secondary School Students' Conventional Expectations and Interpretive Operations', *English in Education*, 41(3): 20–36.

The Poetry Society (2010) *Teaching the Reading of Poetry*, available at: http://www.poetrysociety.org.uk/content/education/reading (accessed 7 April 2010).

QCDA (Qualifications and Curriculum Development Agency) (n.d.) *Cross-curriculum Dimensions: A Planning Guide for Schools*, available at: http://curriculum.qcda.gov.uk/uploads/Cross%20curriculum%20dimensions%20-%20a%20planning%20guide%20for%20schools%20publication_tcm8-14464.pdf (accessed 7 April 2010).

Snapper, G. (2009) 'Editorial', *English Drama Media*, 13: 2–3.

Stephen, M. (1996) *The Price of Pity*. London: Leo Cooper.

Stevens, D. (2005) 'Literacy and Citizenship: An Intercultural Perspective', *Changing English*, 12(2): 253–63.

Stevens, D. (2007) '"Draw Your Own Conclusions": Teaching Pre-twentieth Century Poetry in an Arts Context', *English in Education*, 41(3): 54–66.

Stevenson, R.L. (1885) 'From a Railway Carriage', available, for example, at: http://oldpoetry.com/opoem/show/7657-Robert-Louis-Stevenson-From-A-Railway-Carriage (accessed 7 April 2010).

Strong, L. (1961) 'Poetry in the School', in V. De Sola Pinto (ed.), *The Teaching of English in Schools*. London: Macmillan. pp. 1–16.

Vincent, J. (2005) 'Multimodal Literacies in the School Curriculum: An Urgent Matter of Equity', available at: http://www.formatex.org/micte2005/29.pdf (accessed 22 August 2010).

Wilson, A. (2005) 'The Best Forms in the Best Order? Current Poetry Writing Pedagogy at KS2', *English in Education*, 39(3): 19–31.

Yandell, J. (2003) 'Thoughtless Language, or the Death of Child-centred Education', *Changing English*, 10(1): 5–12.

Zephaniah, B. (1995) 'Talking Turkeys', available at: http://www.benjaminzephaniah.com/content/rhyming.php (accessed 7 April 2010).

Chapter 8

Watching the Words: Drama and Poems

Andy Kempe

CHAPTER OVERVIEW

Some poems are inherently dramatic due to their narrative content or the events, characters, places and emotions that are their subject. Others have the potential for dramatisation because of some aural or visual quality of their poetic form. However, if dramatising poems is to be meaningful and effective children need to be taught something about the art form of drama rather than just being left to their own devices. This chapter explores the learning potential of considering the printed text of a poem as a notation of sound, movement, gesture and use of space. The chapter recognises a progression from simple nursery rhymes to the sophisticated use of poetic language in different types of literature that is mirrored in the journey from infants' clapping games to the dramatic juxtaposition of aural and visual images in theatre and the performing arts.

Watchwords by Roger McGough (1969) was the first book of poetry I ever bought. I had just started at teacher training college and was set an assignment requiring me to select a modern poet and produce a critical analysis of a selection of his/her work. This represented something of a challenge for me! I had written a fair few angst-ridden and appallingly pretentious poems of my own, but given the 'O' and 'A' Level syllabuses both teachers and students were shackled to, my knowledge of poetry was limited to what I had found to be either bum-numbingly incomprehensible (Milton's 'Comus'), prissy twaddle (Wordsworth's 'Daffodils') or ripe for rise-taking (Burns' 'Tam O'Shanter'). I imagine my tale is typical for the time; studying poetry was a desk-bound exercise which generally consisted of attempting, as a whole class, to de-code the piece line by line, image by image, enjambment by caesura. The most quotable lines were written into revision notes and rote learnt for the exam when, by God, you'd make sure you used them whether they were relevant to the question or not!

And so to college and an assignment that I had no idea how to start. With all the focus and prescience of Kingsley Amis' Lucky Jim, I meandered into the college bookshop where McGough's invitingly thin collection veritably leapt into my hands. 'Perfect! This will do nicely!' thought I. Not perhaps the most sensitive or intelligent approach to a literary adventure but as serendipity would have it, and notwithstanding my tutor's comment that, 'This is virgin territory and while some would say your poet is not worth the effort you have expended on him I think it has been a worthwhile exercise', a long and fruitful relationship started that day. To use a whole page and have the words dance over them, as in the title poem of Watchwords (McGough, 1969: 7), seemed almost irreverent, not to mention the cavalier rejection of capital letter and punctuation (E.E. Cummings hadn't yet blipped on my radar). Naïve young thing that I was, I was instantly enamoured with McGough's incessant playfulness and punning.

The way McGough used the page to make visual puns or emphasise meanings was a revelation for me. In the poem 'Watchwords' the words are literally 'up and all over the place', punishing readers who dare to take their eyes off them for a minute. When, later in my first year of teacher training, I undertook my first teaching practice in an inner city primary school and was asked to do a project on the seasons, I knew I would be able to use the mournful 'Snowscene' and blistering 'The Fight of the Year' not as the subject of literary analysis but as scripts to bring to life somehow; to do in the three dimensions of the classroom what McGough was doing on a two-dimensional page.

Several years on I can now see how the poem entitled 'Watchwords' represents so much of what I like about poems and still stands as a case study of how I have approached them with children and students of all ages. In a nutshell, 'watching the words' implies that some poems have a potential that cannot be fully addressed through either reading or recitation, given that both their content and form entice a visual interpretation. When Abbs argues for a dynamic approach to the teaching of poetry he is essentially encouraging teachers to get students to speak the words aloud rather than just reading them. He cites Paul Valéry's edict that poetry 'comes to life only in two situations – in the state of composition in a mind that nominates and constructs it, and in the state of recitation' (Abbs, 1989: 72). More recently, Michael Rosen has made this philosophy manifest through the use of *YouTube* as a medium for inspiring and sharing poetry:

Watching poems being performed is very accessible. The point about poetry is that it is not just about words, it is about tone and rhythm. Experienced readers can get this off the page, but the inexperienced can't. Part of this idea is to try to up the level of interest by showing the physical side of poetry. (*TES*, 2009: 16)

The intention of this chapter is to go one step further than this however and consider how a creative approach to the teaching of poetry might embrace Suzanne Langer's definition of drama as 'poetry in the mode of action' (1953: 322). In doing so I believe we can meet the requirements of the National Curriculum in more creative and productive ways than its authors are likely ever to have envisaged. When, for example, the Programme of Study for English states that:

In coming to understand the author's craft students should understand:

j) how texts are crafted to shape meaning and produce particular effects
k) how writers structure and organise different texts including non-linear and multimodal [sic] (QCA, 2007: 66)

it seems to me that licence is being given to creative approaches that will indeed allow teachers and students to make 'fresh connections between ideas, experiences, texts and words', use 'inventive approaches to making meaning, taking risks, playing with language and using it to create new effects', and employ their imagination 'to convey themes, ideas and arguments' (QCA, 2007: 62).

What this chapter will argue, though, is that it's not 'imagination' that conveys ideas, but the manifestation of the imagination in physical action, that is, through the use of both the voice and the body in space. So, for example, McGough's 'Watchwords' might be brought to life not only by speaking the words aloud, but by positioning the speakers as if the floor was the page and adding movement as suggested by the words. A simple but effective way of illustrating the poem's potential meaning: a literary and literal adaptation of the artist Paul Klee's notion of 'taking a line for a walk'.

I See a Voice

The inspiration I initially took from McGough as a trainee teacher was soon compounded by Michael Rosen's invaluable anthology and classroom resource *I See a Voice* with its liberating edict that, 'Poems are jokes, lessons, speeches, complaints, boasts, hopes, dreams, rumours, insults, gossip, memories, lists. I see each poem I write, each poem I read, each poem I hear as part of a conversation' (1981: 7). Rosen never references the origin of his title yet it seems to me highly pertinent in the context of this chapter. The line comes of course from *A Midsummer Night's Dream* when the inept actor Bottom muddles Pyramus' lines and proclaims:

> I see a voice. Now will I to the chink,
>
> To spy an I can hear my Thisbe's face.

> (Act V, Scene 1)

For the audience, the humour here will rest as much in what the (hopefully competent) actor playing Bottom does while he delivers the lines as it does in the words themselves. The point is that while just speaking words aloud can give poetic language new meanings, suiting the actions to words and the words to the actions in complementary or juxtapositional ways can lead to an infinitely greater array of interpretations.

One way of considering poetic language is to view the words as notation of sound, serving the same function as minims and crochets on a stave. Myra Barrs has suggested that, 'reading aloud becomes a bridge between orality and literacy, the way of demonstrating the tunes on the page,' (Nicholson, 1996: 250). Helen Nicholson takes the point further in discussing ways of bringing Hiawyn Oram's children's book *Angry Arthur* (1993) to life not simply in a re-enactment of the story, but as a re-creation of the narrative 'in a different artistic mode of represen-tation'. Nicholson notes how Oram's language is poetic and makes conscious use of devices such as alliteration, simile and onomatopoeia which 'tempt the reader to vocalise the words, and are rich in the dramatic potential of crescendo and diminuendo'. If the cadences and structure of the language tempt a vocalisation, then some responsibility rests with the teacher to be mindful of Abbs' recognition that 'the oral rendering of texts requires the development of those qualities an actor brings to a script' (1989: 72), and to introduce children to the vocal skills required to bring the printed word to life. What is called for here however is no more than an extension of the playful interactions between adults and infants apparent in clapping games and rhymes such as 'Five Fat Sausages Frying in a Pan', 'Two Little Dicky Birds', or rounds such as this personal favourite:

> I sat next to the Duchess at tea
>
> It was all that I feared it would be
>
> Her rumblings abdominal
>
> Were simply abominable
>
> And everybody thought it was me!

From such beginnings runs a progression in the exploration and exercise of the voice as an instrument. Tongue-twisters such as 'Peter Piper' and Dr Seuss' 'The Grip-Top Sock' (Geisel, 1979) can be used to encourage children to play with rhythm while learning the importance of enunciation. (It's worth noting here that while the idea of 'elocution lessons' with all its class-based connotations may seem anathema to many a contemporary teacher, the word 'elocution' relates simply to the art of speaking clearly and expressively, which seems to me to make such exercises perfectly legitimate (Kempe & Holroyd, 2004: 29)). At KS3 one might use some of the songs from the First World War and, taking the lead from *Oh What a Lovely War* (Theatre Workshop, 1965), explore how the jolly tunes of 'The Bells of Hell go Ting-a-ling-a-ling' and 'Sister Susie's Sewing Shirts for Soldiers' can be starkly contrasted with physicalised visual images of a grave-digging squad at work or women manically sewing: no wonder soldiers 'sent epistles saying they'd sooner sleep on thistles than the saucy soft short shirts for soldiers [i.e. shrouds] that Sister Susie sews.'

Parallel to this line of progression, children of all ages can revel in the sheer delight of stringing words together, as in Gervase Phinn's rhyming and rhythmic eulogy of Yorkshire place names in 'The Biggest and the Best' (Phinn, 1995: 25). Fun can be had using the *Yellow Pages* or *Roget's Thesaurus* as a like resource and Seamus Heaney himself has noted how the 'exotic listing on the wireless dial: Stuttgart, Liepzig, Oslo, Hilversum' and the 'beautiful sprung rhythms of the old BBC weather forecast: Dogger, Rockall, Malin, Shetland ...' played a part in his development as a crafter of words (Benton & Benton, 1995a: 143). While not poetry per se, the craft that writers such as Margaret Mahy exhibit in their stories for children can similarly be used to draw attention to the aesthetics of poetic language. For example, *The Man Whose Mother was a Pirate* contains passages reminiscent of Dylan Thomas' 'Holiday Memory' (1954):

Suddenly there was the sea. The little man could only stare. He hadn't dreamed of the BIGNESS of the sea. He hadn't dreamed of the blueness of it. He hadn't thought it would roll like kettledrums, and swish itself on the beach. He opened his mouth, and the drift and the dream of it, the weave and the wave of it, the fume and the foam of it never left him again. At his feet the sea stroked the sand with soft little paws. Farther out, the great, graceful breakers moved like kings into court, trailing the peacock-patterned sea behind them. (Mahy, 1985: not numbered)

Passages such as this are ideal for introducing primary aged children to some simple choral speaking techniques. As a whole class or in small groups they can be tasked to highlight those words and phrases that strike them as being especially important or evocative. Thereafter they can experiment with how to give a rendition of the passage greater texture by speaking some words altogether in *chorus*, using one or more voices to *echo* selected words spoken by the primary speaker (the *coryphaeus*, to use the Ancient Greek term for the leader of the Chorus), or having a string of echoes (*canon*). With secondary school aged students, exactly the same technique can be used to give insights into the structural and stylistic devices such as repetition, metre and metaphor in popularly studied poems such as Vernon Scannell's 'A Case of Murder' (1998). The techniques are similarly useful in making Shakespeare's language seem more vibrant and accessible.

Preparing young voices to speak poetry clearly and expressively doesn't just require attending to diction but also volume. Getting children to bring McGough's 'Pantomime Poem' (1971: 35) to life as a class or working in pairs on Roger Stevens' 'Louder!' (Figure 8.1) (1996) are good resources to employ here, though possibly not when the class next door are doing their SATs tests.

Louder!

OK, Andrew, nice and clearly – off you go.

Welcome everybody to our school concert …

Louder, please, Andrew. Mums and dads won't hear you at the back, will they?

Welcome everybody to our school concert …

Louder, Andrew. You're not trying.
Pro – ject – your – voice.
Take a b i g   b r e a t h   and louder!

Welcome everybody to our school concert …

For goodness sake, Andrew. LOUDER! LOUDER!

Welcome every body to our school concert!

Now, Andrew, there's no need to be silly.

Roger Stevens

Figure 8.1   'Louder!'

Physicalisation

Using a poem such as 'Louder!' as a dramatic script involves a degree of physicalisation by proxy in that by using the size of the font as an intra-dialogic instruction to determine the relative volume with which each line should be delivered necessarily involves a degree of physical control. What tends to happen as a quite natural by-product is that children begin to become animated in terms of facial expression, gesture and use of space. Getting the children to recognise and discuss this contributes to their understanding of the dynamics of speaking and listening and develops an appreciation of the fact that live oral communication involves a good deal of visual signalling. This paves the way to more considered dramatic representations. If, in the pursuit of exploring the relationship between drama and poetry, we are to consider words as notation of potential performance rather than an end in themselves, then we need to be mindful of the polysemic nature of the act of live communication. In other words, when a speaker/performer is communicating with a listener/audience, there is such an abundance of visual and aural signs being imparted that it would be impossible to notate them all. As Jonathan Miller (1986: 45) points out, 'the phonetic distinctions that can make a difference to the meaning of a sentence are so small that it would take an almost infinite set of written characters to represent them all'. If one adds to this all of the other elements that make up a recitation/performance, such as the acoustics and spatial dynamics of the auditorium, the performers' use of space and proximity to the audience, not to mention the deliberate or unintentional use of costume, lighting and scenic background, one becomes aware of both the complexity of casual communication and the creativity and artistry involved in deliberate performance.

There are useful lessons and transferable skills for young people to learn here but there is no need to be intimidated by their apparent intricacies. The answer, it seems to me, is to use short, simple poems as a vehicle for introducing children to their almost limitless possibilities. Two pieces that I have always found capable of facilitating rich discussion are these clerihews by John Foster:

> Neil Armstrong
> Wasn't on the Moon for long.
> But in that time he left behind
> A giant footprint for mankind.

> Count Dracula
> At blood-sports is quite spectacular.
> He hunts for prey at dead of night
> And always gets in the first bite. (In Foster, 2007: 256)

Giving children no more than five minutes to work in groups of between three and five in order to 'act out' the lines using movement, facial expression, gesture and whatever vocal techniques they have already been taught, can pro-duce enormously pleasing work. Such outcomes deserve careful reflection on how dramatisation of the poetic language itself creates both new insights into the words on the page and new meanings that can only be ascribed to the per-formance given. It also, clearly, introduces the possibility of considering visual images as a form of poetry, an enterprise endorsed by the Bentons. In *Double Vision,* for example, they equate the development of visual literacy through 'reading' paintings for meaning with the growing appreciation of poetry, as 'our attention moves from detail to detail as we build up our first impressions' (Benton & Benton, 1990: 8). *Double Vision* captures the conversations that are possible between pictures and poems. By giving examples of how pictures have inspired poems, it paves the way for turning this around and exploring poems by creating visual images for them. This technique is only touched upon explicitly in one example in *Double Vision* which suggests making a storyboard of extracts of 'The Rime of the Ancient Mariner' (p. 72). The storyboard technique can, however, be quite easily adapted into the physical activity of making sequences of still images to illustrate narrative poems such as 'Flannan Isle' or 'The Highwayman'. Students working at KS3 and KS4 may use more sophisticated physical theatre techniques such as Rudolf Laban's 'efforts' (Newlove, 1993) or Jacques Lecoq's 'states of tension' (2009) to plot abstract sequences encapsulat-ing the emotional movement suggested in the poem's words.

Performing Poems

In *Painting with Words*, the Bentons rightly state that: 'Reproductions are infor-mation, not art ... [nonetheless] Reproduced images are valuable as ways-in' (1995b: 5). In the same way, a performance of a poem is just that, a perform-ance, not the poem itself. It is the result of interpretation and mediation into a physical form, yet the performance of a poem can serve as an invaluable and intriguing 'way-in'. By way of example, allow me to describe a simple lesson using Pieter Bruegel's painting *Children's Games* and William Carlos Williams' poem on the same subject (Benton & Benton, 1990: 82–5).

In the first instance the class look carefully at the picture either on a hard copy or projected through a data projector. They are asked to offer words and phrases which relate to the picture. Each student finds a space and assumes the position of a character in the picture (it doesn't matter if two or more students appear to have chosen the same figure to represent). On a given signal, the pic-ture is spontaneously brought to life through movement and sound for around 30 seconds. The students reflect on what was achieved in terms of atmosphere. Each student is given a verse from William Carlos Williams' poem. The verses will need to have been numbered beforehand according to how many there are in the class. There are 22 verses so either some students may be given two to read or some verses will be read by more than one voice. The class stand in a circle and rehearse the reading so that each student knows who will speak before them and so act as their cue. The scene is set in motion once more but with only muted improvised sound. One by one the players freeze and read aloud their verse but then continue to add a quiet background soundscape. By the last verse of the poem all the students should be standing in a tableau akin to the painting. Fade the soundscape out and allow the image to sink in for a moment. In reflecting on the scene they have created, the students consider this exercise both as a piece of theatre in its own right but also what new insight into the poem and painting it has afforded them. This sort of work is obviously highly orientated towards honing performance skills but can encourage pupils to consider the potential of other poems for this kind of treatment.

Turning narrative poems or those containing clear visual imagery into performance pieces is relatively easy and may have the end result of a pleasing performance reflecting a heightened appreciation of the poem. However, one of the problems teachers encounter with a good deal of poetry is that both content and structure may appear abstruse to their pupils. I will not pretend to have a simple answer to this, though am willing to re-state my belief that simply attending to the sounds of individual words and the way whole lines run together can help students make sense of them far more quickly than giving lengthy explanations of their semantic meaning (Kempe & Ashwell (2000): 117–18). Many a teacher has killed not only the odd poem but entire Shakespeare plays stone dead by interrupting a reading after virtually every word to explain what it all means or ponder what the author really meant. Better by far just to read longer sections aloud with a class, placing an emphasis on the actual sounds being made and then discussing what seems to be the gist of the thing. Consider, for example, this extract from *Hamlet* (Act 1, Scene 5):

> ... sleeping within my orchard,
>
> My custom always of the afternoon,
>
> Upon my secure hour thy uncle stole
>
> With juice of cursed hebona in a vial,
>
> And in the porches of my ears did pour
>
> The leperous distilment; whose effect
>
> Hold such an enmity with blood of man
>
> That swift as quicksilver it courses through
>
> The natural gates and alleys of the body,
>
> And with sudden vigour it doth posset
>
> And curd, like eager droppings into milk,
>
> The thin and wholesome blood. So did it mine.

Reading this passage aloud and listening to the sounds of the words and where the pauses are reveals a lot about what is happening. Notice the ponderous rhythm of the first two lines compared to the sense of creeping step by step in line 3. The effect of the poison is described in one long breath reflecting how it does indeed attack the body 'swift as quicksilver', whereas the line 'posset and curd, like eager droppings' seems to demand a slower delivery which sends the whole face into a paroxysm; the line neither sounds or looks at all pleasant when delivered by children delighting in being repulsive!

What is needed are ways of getting children to trust their own ability to make sense out of sounds which may at first seem alien to them. My favourite ploy with young teenagers is to use 'Karawane' by the Dadaist poet Hugo Ball for this (Figure 8.2).

KARAWANE
jolifanto bambla ô falli bambla
grossiga m'pfa habla horem
égiga goramen
higo bloiko russula huju
hollaka hollala
anlogo bung
blago bung
blago bung
bosso fataka
ü üü ü
schampa wulla wussa ólobo
hej tatta gôrem
eschige zunbada
wulubu ssubudu uluw ssubudu
tumba ba- umf
kusagauma
ba - umf

Figure 8.2 'Karawane'

The poem is handed out and read aloud in as neutral a voice as possible. The pupils discuss how the different typefaces may suggest tone and volume. They should also consider how the punctuation and sounds of words might suggest mood. Working in groups of five or six, the pupils are encouraged to read the poem aloud several times over, commenting on each others' delivery as they attempt to read the words phonetically. The next step is to contextualise the piece. The clue here is in the title, so ask the pupils to suggest situations surrounding a desert caravan. For example, simply riding in the camel train in the heat of the day; bartering for goods in the old bazaar in Cairo; loading up the camels in the morning after a night in the open; sitting saddle sore around a camp fire. Given such a context, each group considers the different sorts of characters suggested by the lines and 'casts' the text accordingly. The students rehearse the scene, speaking the lines in the order in which they are printed and attempting to convey the context for the 'conversation' and the relationship between the speakers as clearly as possible. In this way, guided by the typography and their own imaginations, sense emerges from what the pupils at first would have seen as nothing but nonsense. Such a lesson provides valuable insights into the relationship between the sounds of words and their potential meanings, reflecting Abbs' assertion that 'the poem has as many meanings as the voice can render with artistic effect' (1989: 73).

The Poetry of Drama

To some extent, the discussion above around the relationship between drama and poetry has suggested that drama may be a useful 'way in' to poetry. Such an assertion needs further consideration. Certainly, exercises wherein physical actions are used alongside vocal renditions of the words may stand by themselves as engaging, fun activities which contribute to a growing aesthetic awareness. They may also provide children with insights into the nature and outcomes of the acts of interpretation and communication, and these too are worthwhile by-products. To what extent, though, does such work genuinely contribute to an understanding of the poem as a poem? At the risk of sounding too much like the teacher trainer I am, the activities teachers choose to undertake with their classes need to be governed by clear objectives. In this case, teachers need to be clear in their own minds about the relationship between two distinctly different art forms: there's drama, and there's poetry. Poems may be inherently dramatic or hold the potential for dramatisation, and drama may be poetic in its use of language and other visual and aural signifiers. Drama and poetry may complement each other but they are not synonymous and are governed by distinguishably different systems of structure and interpretation. Langer's analysis of the relationship between words and music provides a helpful parallel in understanding this:

> When words and music come together in song, music swallows words; not only mere words and literal sentences, but even literary word-structures, poetry ... Song is not a compromise between poetry and music, though the text taken by itself may be a great poem; song is music ... when a composer puts a poem to music, he annihilates the poem and makes a song. (1953: 152–3)

In the same vein, one may argue that when a poem is performed the visual and aural elements of the performance swallow the words, or rather the words become just one part of a greater whole. In performing the poem, we do not so much annihilate the poem but create a new, polysemic, piece of poetry. It's interesting to note here that Langer recognises how some composers, such as Beethoven, were excited by great literature while others found a musical core in seemingly insignificant verses. She cites Schubert's use of Müller's work which, while not greatly rated for its literary quality, served just as well as text because 'in the musical works to which they have given rise their inferiority is redeemed, because as poetry they have disappeared' (Langer 1953: 153).

According to Langer, drama is:

> [a] poetic art, because it creates the primary illusion of all poetry – virtual history. Its substance is an image of human life – ends, means, gains and losses, fulfilment and decline and death. It is a fabric of illusory experience, and that is the essential product of poesis. (p. 306)

Thus, the teacher's objective may be to use a poem as a springboard for creating a piece of drama or, conversely, he/she may employ techniques of dramatisation to interrogate aspects of the poem. While the ultimate product of either approach may well be to create, re-create or reflect on images of human life, the teacher may well also wish his/her class to examine more closely the mechanics by which such images are generated.

The Drama of Poetry

Although there seems to be a general acknowledgement that drama can be an effective way of engaging children with poetry, guidance for teachers on just how to put the two art forms together in order to facilitate learning is not as plentiful as one might expect. For example, the preface of the Bentons' *Poetry Workshop* (1995a) promises 'a varied programme of discussion, drama, and creative and critical thinking', yet the only direct reference to drama thereafter is in the vague claim that 'some of the poems and pictures might suggest situations and themes for improvisation' (p. 20). Similarly, Phinn (1995: 4–5) lists things that teachers might do to encourage children to enjoy, appreciate and understand poetry, for example, 'performing their own poems and published verse in the classroom and at assembly' yet he gives no explicit guidance on how to make performances effective or productive in terms of learning about or through the poems that are performed. By contrast, teachers may find the work of contemporary drama educators rather more inspirational. For example, Grainger and Cremin (2001: 19–23) describe how a complete 'process drama' was evolved from just one image of a ship suggested by John Cotton's poem 'Through That Door'. Similarly, Winston (2000: 14–26) offers lively ideas for exploring the morality which underpins *Tinker Jim* by Gillian Maclure and Paul Coleman, while Tandy (2003: 151–6) describes how John Walsh's poem 'The Bully Asleep' provided the basis for a piece of theatre examining the issue of bullying. The intentions here however are clearly to use the content of the poems as stimuli for drama. Baldwin and Fleming (2003: 96–104) likewise employ a range of drama strategies such as hot seating, role play and 'conscience alley' to work through the narrative of Tennyson's 'The Lady of Shallott'. In some contrast however, Ackroyd and Boulton (2001: 98–102) pay greater attention to the verbal imagery of this poem by getting the children to firstly create physical interpretation of the images, then reflect on how the visual and verbal articulate with each other.

Some poems capture a moment of drama through the use of direct speech and as such offer younger students the opportunity to illustrate the moment through their embodiment of character and situation. Examples of poems that may be used in this way include 'Miller's End' by Charles Causley (1970: 82–3) and Michael Rosen's 'The Car Trip' (1998). It is important that teachers read new texts aloud to a class in the first instance so that the children become familiar with the narrative content of the poem without being distracted or worried by words they are unable to read fluently for themselves. Teachers need, of course, to be proficient at reading aloud themselves, thus modelling the way tone, pitch and volume can make the text sound interesting. Having done this, the pupils can work in pairs or appropriately sized groups to read the poem aloud, taking alternate lines. Some students will automatically start to put some character into their voices and this should be encouraged. In moving towards a presentation, it's best to encourage the pupils not to get bogged down with trying to be too naturalistic – four classroom chairs will do for a car and there's more fun to be had using bodies and voices to make sound effects than employing pre-recorded sources. It's a good constraint to insist that none of the lines of the poem are changed and no new lines are added. Some students may of course put too much action and noise into their work, with the result that the presentation will be cluttered and chaotic. Draw attention to this and go on to explore possible ways of editing movement and sounds in order to keep the focus tighter on the original text. Despite the moans and groans that may occur, it is rarely a productive use of time to have every single group showing work of this nature. In fact, showing six or more similar versions of the same thing will just become tedious for students and teachers alike. In terms of advancing learning it is more useful to watch just one or two groups who have interpreted the task in very different ways then invite the rest of the class to comment on how the work compares and contrasts.

Content and Form

While for Langer the essential product of poesis, whether in the form of drama or poetry itself, may be the imaging of the substance of human life, teachers of both drama and poetry are charged with helping pupils acquire an understanding of how such images are brought about and, one would hope, inspiring the pupils themselves to create their own poetic images through the respective art forms. In this project I have found it helpful to constantly refer back to three basic questions:

- *What is being said?* That is, what's the content?
- *How is it being said?* Or rather, what's the form?
- *Is it any good?* Put simply, what is your response?

There are a range of drama-based techniques which offer a 'way in' to poems and address all three of these questions in order to help students arrive at a considered critical and imaginative response.

To explore the *content* one might use educational drama strategies such as:

- *Role on the wall*: to 'fill out' the key characters of narrative- or character-based poems by giving them a backstory.
- *Hot seating*: to explore characters' motivation or perspective.
- *Thought tracking/conscience alley*: to consider why characters do as they do and what choices they believe they have.
- *Role play*: to explore the events of the poem from different perspectives and consider where such events may have originated and what their consequences were.
- *Forum theatre*: to 're-write' the narrative in order to explore what a more satisfactory outcome may be for both the characters and the audience.

These methods can help pupils 'make contact' with the world of the poem and be helpful in generating creative responses in drama and written work. However, if poems are, as Coleridge puts it, 'the best words in the best order', pupils should also explore how the poet has conveyed the content through the use of form; as A.E. Housman (1933: 37) put it: 'Poetry is not the thing said but a way of saying it'. This implies focusing on devices such as alliteration, assonance and dissonance, rhyme and rhythm, mood and tone, diction and metre. These very same devices occur in dramatic literature, of course, which suggests to me that there is all the more reason to study drama and poetry in conjunction with each other and so give the lie to Hazlitt's proclamation that, 'poetry and the stage do not agree well together' (1817: 92).

SOMETHING TO THINK ABOUT

How can you integrate more closely the poetry and drama activities you currently teach? What could working with poems add to your pupils' learning in drama? What could using drama add to your pupils' learning in poetry?

SOMETHING TO READ

The other chapters in this book have valuable things to say about the teaching of poetry and offer a wealth of ideas regarding poems that are worth studying. This chapter has suggested a few books which teachers may draw on to develop their understanding of how to employ drama in their teaching. In addition, Chapter 7 of Michael Fleming's excellent book *Starting Drama Teaching* (David Fulton, 2003) provides clear guidance on dramatic approaches to texts including poems.

SOMETHING TO DO

- Introduce your pupils to the term *positioning*. This term is used in the theatre to describe how an audience is made to think and feel about the characters or situation in the drama. A key question for children to ask in any process of dramatisation therefore ought to be, 'what do we want the audience to get from this?' Asking such a question will help the pupils stay focused as it will guide the artistic decisions they are making and so give greater insights into the potential of the content and form they are working with.
- What are the practical implications of this chapter in terms of your own teaching situation? Would it be necessary to find a special space to implement the ideas proposed here, or how might you either adapt the ideas or adapt your usual teaching space in order to try them out?

References

Abbs, P. (1989) *A is for Aesthetic*. Lewes: Falmer Press.

Ackroyd, J. & Boulton, J. (2001) *Drama Lessons for Five- to Eleven-Year-Olds*. London: David Fulton.

Baldwin, P. & Fleming, K. (2003) *Teaching Literacy through Drama*. London: Routledge.

Benton, M. & Benton, P. (1990) *Double Vision*. London: Hodder & Stoughton.

Benton, M. & Benton, P. (1995a) *Poetry Workshop*. London: Hodder & Stoughton.

Benton, M. & Benton, P. (1995b) *Painting with Words*. London: Hodder & Stoughton.

Causley, C. (1970) *Figgie Hobbin*. Basingstoke: Macmillan.

Cookson, P. (2000) *The Works*. Basingstoke: Macmillan.

Foster, J. (2007) *The Poetry Chest*. Oxford: Oxford University Press.

Geisel, T.S. (Dr Seuss) (1979) *O Say Can You Say*. New York: Beginner Books.

Grainger, T. & Cremin, M. (2001) *Classroom Drama 5–8*. Sheffield: NATE.

Hazlitt, W. (1817) *Characters of Shakespeare's Plays*. London: Templeman.

Housman, A.E. (1933) *The Name and Nature of Poetry*. Cambridge: Cambridge University Press.

Kempe, A. & Ashwell, M. (2000) *Progression in Secondary Drama*. Oxford: Heinemann.

Kempe, A. & Holroyd, J. (2004) *Speaking, Listening and Drama*. London: David Fulton.

Langer, S. (1953) *Feeling and Form*. London: Routledge & Kegan Paul.

Lecoq, J. (2009) *The Moving Body*. London: Methuen.

McGough, R. (1969) *Watchwords*. London: Jonathan Cape.

McGough, R. (1971) *After the Merrymaking*. London: Jonathan Cape.

Mahy, M. (1985) *The Man Whose Mother Was a Pirate*. London: Dent.

Miller, J. (1986) *Subsequent Performances*. London: Faber.

Newlove, J. (1993) *Laba for Actors and Dancers*. London: Nick Hern Books.

Nicholson, H. (1996) 'Voices on Stage', in M. Styles, E. Bearne & V. Watson (eds) *Voices Off*. London: Cassell.

Oram, H. (1993) *Angry Arthur*. London: Andersen Press.

Phinn, G. (1995) *Touches of Beauty: Teaching Poetry in the Primary School*. Doncaster: Rosela Publications.

Qualifications & Curriculum Authority (QCA) (2007) *The National Curriculum: Statutory Requirements for Key Stages 3 and 4*. London: QCA.

Rosen, M. (1981) *I See a Voice*. London: Thames/Hutchinson.

Rosen, M. (1998) *The Hypnotiser*. London: HarperCollins.

Scannell, V. (1998) *Collected Poems 1950–93*. London: Robson Books.

Stevens, R. (1996) 'Louder!', in B. Moses (ed.), *Performance Poems*. Crediton: Southgate

Tandy, M. (2003) 'Dreaming for Good: Drama and Personal and Social Development', in S. Inman, M. Buck & M. Tandy, *Enhancing Personal, Social and Health Education*. London: Routledge Falmer.

Theatre Workshop (1965) *Oh What a Lovely War*. London: Methuen.

Thomas, D. (1954) *Quite Early One Morning*. London: Dent.

Times Educational Supplement (TES) (2009) 'Rosen Shows that Rhyme Does Pay: New Poetry YouTube Encourages Pupils' Reading through Safe Online Showcase', 20 November.

Winston, J. (2000) *Drama, Literacy and Moral Education 5–11*. London: David Fulton.

Chapter 9

'Literary Reading': The Challenge of Getting Young People to Experience Poetry

Andy Goodwyn

CHAPTER OVERVIEW

In recent years a strong emphasis has been placed on learning how to analyse the formal properties of poetry, especially for examination and test purposes. As a result, one of the challenges for teachers has been finding ways to encourage students to enjoy the emotional and personal power of poetry. This chapter, based on research with poetry classes and teachers at Key Stages 2 and 3, argues for the importance and benefits of adopting a 'literary reading' approach to poems, where students spend significant time on individual poems and generate a range of responses, both personal and creative. Also emphasised is the importance of recognising the value of reader response theory for all teachers, as a conceptual framework in which literary reading can take place. This combined approach develops the confidence and enthusiasm of young readers to engage with poetry and to avoid the urge merely to 'solve the riddle' of the poem.

The Flat Historic Scale?

In Wallace Stevens' 'Le Monocle of Mon Oncle' (Stevens, 1965: 10–11) the cynical and depressed narrator laments his and his partner's ageing bodies, beginning: 'Our bloom is gone –'. Unfortunately many experienced English teachers may feel the same after over 20 years of domineering and reductive curricula and testing regimes. Where are the exotic fruits of poetry and the brilliant blues of creativity of Stevens' poem in the Framework for English? There is no question that the teaching of poetry has suffered particularly over that long, 20-year period. Ironically a recent survey of secondary English teachers asking them to consider the current status and purpose of teaching literature in schools (Goodwyn, 2010) produced at least one deeply depressing finding: the great majority thought there was far too much poetry in Key Stage 4. Given that poetry is both part of the National Curriculum and features clearly in all the various forms of GCSE available, this would suggest that these guardians of literature had simply had enough of teaching poetry; are they now just 'Yeomen' in Stevens' terms? However, a closer examination of this finding, especially through an analysis of comments, reveals a very different issue:

> Poetry dominates my teaching but for all the wrong reasons. I spend ages on each of the anthology poems and my students become very familiar with them but they also lose all real interest in them as poems, it is all about the exam answer.

> I used to love teaching poetry – now I actually dread it on some days, having to drag through the same poem as last year with the same reluctant students.

> Although there seems to be lots of poetry – which ought to be a good thing – what there really is, is lots of assessing of kids' secondhand ideas about poems that they have to study. (Goodwyn, unpublished research)

What these teachers are saying is firstly that they spend far too much time didactically presenting poems that their students must produce timed answers about, in hot summer examination rooms. Secondly they find themselves teaching these poems every year in the same way and losing all sense of them as poems per se. Finally they have to ensure that their students can discuss the formal and linguistic characteristics of each poem and can make explicit use of technical terminology. They identify that all literature teaching in KS4 is now dominated by analytical approaches to text with very little opportunity to allow for creative responses and even less for personal interpretations.

It is, therefore, worth playing 'the historic scale', in Wallace Stevens' phrase, to see if the music of poetry in school has always sounded so flat. English teachers and primary teachers have certainly felt like mere yeomen at times but the past offers them real hope for a better future.

We shall start with the present scenario and then escape it for a glimpse of better times. It might be argued that Key Stages 2 and 3 have always had more flexibility and were less dominated by the very specific demands of GCSE, especially GCSE Literature examinations. However, English teachers always found the KS3, Year 9, test desperately restrictive with a wash back effect through Years 8 and 7 (Goodwyn, 2010). At Key Stage 2, primary teachers found the effect of the Literacy Hour and the Strategies equally restrictive. This is not to suggest that good teachers were not teaching poetry with enthusiasm and success in their individual classrooms, what it reveals is that such teaching, in spite of the prevailing ethos, was foisted onto primary and secondary schools by the National Literacy Strategy and the Framework for English. One purpose of this book is to look ahead beyond these educational juggernauts as they begin to fall apart under their own weight and to anticipate a more creative period for teachers and young people.

It is pertinent here to state briefly that it was not ever thus. The NLS really began in 1997 and the previous nine years of the NC for English did promote better opportunities with poetry, although even those were more a feature of the first three years than the subsequent six, and this was true of primary as well as secondary schools. Although secondary English teachers successfully boycotted the SAT exams for several years, they were outmanoeuvred in the end. In a sense, what this reveals is that from about 1992 onwards, teachers who cared about poetry found it harder and harder to find space to teach it in a way that made their students care for poetry.

Briefly going back further reveals a very different era. In the 1980s teachers had real freedom to choose what suited them and their students. There was no NC, no Ofsted, and the 1980s secondary schools were dominated by the new GCSE, the 'common' exam for all abilities that strongly emphasised a course-work approach and teacher assessment. Students were able to select poems to write about and to produce creative responses of all kinds. They could write their own poems and include them in portfolios of work which teachers could then assess using externally determined criteria, but not dominated by a pre-scriptive test. Primary schools had real freedom to select poetry suitable to their locality and the cultures and languages of all their children.

This way of working was developed in the 1960s and 1970s. In primary schools this was the era of progressive education and themed working that generated endless opportunities for children to read and write poetry and to display it in their classrooms (Dias and Hayhoe, 1988). In secondary schools the development of the Certificate of Secondary Education (CSE), the examination for all children who had failed the eleven-plus exam, was truly innovative. It broke away totally from the 'Ordinary' ('O') level model of essay writing and comprehension and brought in speaking and listening and, for this chapter most importantly, creative writing and, what I would call, 'creative reading'. By 'creative reading' is meant a form of reading where the response to that reading could be in many creative modes. A simple example would be that, having read a poem, a student might respond with a poem of their own, a picture, a piece of drama, a story, and so on; that is, using their imaginative and creative powers. There were plenty of opportunities for more formal analytical responses, discussions, critiques and essays and so on, but these forms were part of an extensive repertoire of multi-faceted responses. What the 'historic scale' reveals is that teaching poetry can be genuinely about developing the responses of children and young people and can make engaging with poetry a meaningful experience for them.

Readers Responding

At the heart of this chapter lies the notion of response, that is what the individual reader experiences as a result of reading and re-reading the poem, or equally from hearing and re-hearing a poem. Louise Rosenblatt's pioneering work and two seminal texts, *Literature as Exploration* (1938) and *The Reader, the Text, the Poem* (1978) are as powerful today as when they were first written. At one level her work can be counterpointed against the New Critics who argued that individual readers were a problem and a distraction (Dias & Hayhoe, 1988), and that there was a single interpretation to be found in a poem, which was the purpose in reading and analysing any poetic text and the fundamental raison d'être of criticism. Rosenblatt stated:

> The special meanings, and, more particularly, the submerged associations that these words and images have for the individual reader will largely determine what the work communicates to him. The reader brings to the work personality traits, memories of past events, present needs and preoccupations, a particular mood of the moment, and a particular physical condition. These and many other elements in a never-to-be-duplicated combination determine his response to the peculiar contribution of the text. (Rosenblatt, 1938: 30–1)

There are three key points in her concept of what has become known as 'reader response theory' (RRT). The poem is brought into existence when being read, therefore it is an event which is experienced by the individual, its meaning is dynamic and open to constant reinterpretations. As Richard Beach argues in his excellent book *A Teacher's Introduction to Reader Response Theories* (1993) there has been much subsequent thinking and RRT is no more a unified theory than any other comparable field, postmodernism being a good example. What does unify the theory, and make it so valuable to teachers, is its absolute focus on the reader and on its celebration of individual response. The key pedagogical implication is that the reader must be enabled to respond as an individual. This does not however imply merely that 'anything goes'. It implies that a reader will try to interpret a poem using all mental resources including personal memory and association; this therefore means that a poem can resonate very differently with each reader. However, this does not trap a reader in a hermetically sealed vault of isolation. On the contrary, in trying to create a meaning from the experience of the poem, readers can benefit hugely from the interpretations of others and, very rapidly, realise that a personal association that they had thought was relevant, actually was not.

Another vitally important implication for teaching is the initial privileging of personal, individual response for young readers. In another excellent text, *Developing Response to Poetry* (Dias & Hayhoe, 1988), which is one of the best guides on how to develop an RRT pedagogy, the authors make a simple analogy that far too often students only rent the poems, they never own them; in that sense, because the teachers hurry students into making a definitive interpretation that (typically) agrees with their own, the students do not feel that the poem has possessed them. One more key point from Rosenblatt (1938: Chapter 1) was her very helpful distinction between *efferent* and *aesthetic* modes of reading. In the efferent mode we are 'taking away' from the text some information and this can be as true of poetry as for a guide book. In the aesthetic mode readers are fully engaged as a whole person seeking out the significance of the textual experience and establishing a meaning. Rosenblatt conceptualises these modes as more of a spectrum than as alternatives, with readers constantly employing both stances, but the aesthetic mode is when 'literary reading' takes place.

Literary Reading

The actual nature of the reading of literature has had a very specific focus as a psychological phenomenon in the last 30 years; this development should be seen as complementary to RRT rather than a development from it. It can be traced to the work of I.A. Richards in his seminal *Practical Criticism: A Study of Literary Judgement* (Richards, 1929) when he experimented with Cambridge undergraduates and was struck by 'the astonishing variety of human responses' (Richards, 1929: 12), leading him to identify 10 difficulties common to readers when responding to literature. Two of these are worth noting here. He acknowledges that visual imagery is ambiguous, especially in poetry, because 'we differ immensely in our capacity to visualise' (p. 14), but argues that 'mnemonic irrelevances – misleading effects of the reader's being reminded of some personal scene or reminder' (p. 15) are an obstacle to interpretation. These are different psychological points but they have in common the need for readers to be reflexive and to examine whether their responses are irrelevant or whether their limited reading of an image is sufficient. In other words this is not a difficulty in Richards' negative sense, it is an affordance of reading poetic text. Readers need to 'hold' in their mind that numerous interpretations are valuable, especially in the early stages of creating meaning and in ascertaining significance; this requires frequent opportunities in order for this capacity to develop in all readers.

Recent research (Miall, 2006) suggests that what readers seek is 'significance' in a text; that is what is meaningful to that reader. This sense of 'significance' is one of the key insights of recent attempts to study readers empirically, to try to ascertain the nature of readers' specific experience of reading literature (not just poetry). Firstly, the evidence so far does suggest that 'literary reading' is a very distinct form of reading (see especially Miall, 2006, for a detailed analysis). Secondly, it is increasingly clear that literary language is a specialised form of language, and that human beings value and recognise it. Perhaps paradoxically, it is not especially important to spend huge amounts of time and energy defining literature in order to separate it from other language forms, it is more important to see that human beings can read in a 'literary way', leading to a specific kind of psychological experience. Thirdly, a more recent argument (for example see Carroll, 2004) is that literature in general is part of our evolutionary development and one sign of our most sophisticated adaptation of language. Language is a paramount tool in human development and literature is a key and specific adaptation of that tool. How does this help us teach poetry to children?

It helps us first to see that reading poetry is a very special activity and literally a special form of experience. As real engagement and absorption with poetry is a *special state of mind,* then certain material and psychological elements are important, and these will be considered below. Essentially the stimulus of reading poetry, in that evolutionary sense, is *developmental;* we are using a linguistic tool to work with a specialised form of knowledge. As with all tools, we need constant use to become skilled. Using the tool often will be more important than self-consciously being shown how to use it. What is needed is a balance between 'deliberated practice', for example identifying rhymes, and 'normal use', for example experiencing rhymes and just enjoying rhyming poems.

The Reader Response Classroom

What then are the key ideas that can guide us when teaching to enable children and young people to develop authentic responses to poetry?

- Literature is a special form of knowledge expressed through language.
- The poetic form of language is an even more specialised form than literature.
- Authentic reading of literature is experiential.
- Literary reading is a particular psychological state.
- Literary reading is characterised by an intense, emotional and subjective engagement with a text, when the reader is temporarily 'lost' in the text.
- Responses can veer usefully between efferent and aesthetic.
- The aesthetic approach is key to developing a reader's personal and emotional engagements with a text.

- The poem must be treated as an 'event', it 'happens' when a reader (or listener) is engaged with a poem.
- Creating an optimal classroom climate for engagement is crucial.
- Any response can be important.
- Initial responses are speculative (not 'wrong') and a vital stage in exploring potential meanings (this is as true of adults as of toddlers).
- Responses can be increasingly refined, this requires time and multiple 'events'.
- Responses can come in many modes, and adopting a range of modes enables deeper responses.
- Responsive readers gradually learn to tolerate increasing levels of uncertainty and ambiguity in their initial responses.
- Responsive readers become increasingly engaged by the possibility of multiple and even conflicting interpretations, and therefore increasingly interested in the responses of others.
- Being responsive is emotionally demanding; we are all tempted at times to 'resist' engagement, since being unresponsive at times is normal.
- An authentic response can be enabled but it cannot be forced.
- Students of all ages need to 'own' the poem and their responses, not to 'rent' them from the teacher.
- The teacher's role remains vital but too early an intervention in meaning-making may severely limit students' own capacity to fully engage with a poem.
- If students consistently expect the teacher to define meanings they will not develop the capacity to generate real response and will want to be told 'the right answer'.
- The teacher needs to authentically value the responses of all students and to make this explicit.
- Readers are seeking for 'significance' in a text, therefore they may recognise the 'worth' or 'merit' of a text but not find it significant to them.
- Responsive readers become increasingly reflexive, recognising their own limitations and understanding that what is significant to them may not be so for others, even accepting that texts can become significant to them because the responses of others expand their capacity to find significance.
- Although made up of many individual responses, the reader response classroom becomes a 'community of interpretation'.

Making it Happen

In setting out some very practical examples for the classroom, I am first going to suggest a range of *types of experiential response* and suggested activities, then a range of creative responses that any teacher can adapt. Finally I will consider how making use of such a range of activities in a consistent way will create the optimal climate for readers to enjoy literary reading and become authentic responders to poetry. As the emphasis in this practical section is on an approach to poetry, rather than certain poems, there will be no references to specific poems. It is also important to state that, wherever possible, teachers and students are actively seeking out and selecting poems to bring to the classroom; it is vital that the teacher stays 'fresh' and does not overly rely on the 'tried and tested'.

As mentioned above, RRT is not a unified field and it continues to develop, however for the purposes of this chapter we are going to focus on the processes of experiential response and I am both summarising and adapting material from a great deal of theoretical work and research undertaken in primary and secondary classrooms (see Beach, 1993; Beach & Marshall, 1990; Dias & Hayhoe, 1988; Langer, 1995; Purves & Beach, 1972).

The Processes of Experiential Response

- *Engaging*: emotional involvement, empathising and identifying with the text
- *Constructing*: entering into the world of the text and creating alternative worlds, conceptualising characters, events, settings, atmospheres and moods
- *Imaging*: creating visual images
- *Sounding*: hearing the rhythm and sound structures of the text, becoming sensitive to the aural web, for example the assonance of a text, finding the 'music' of the poem
- *Embodying*: feeling the energy or emotion of the text in a visceral sense
- *Connecting*: relating one's life experience to the current text
- *Evaluating/reflecting*: being self-reflexive about one's engagement with the text, asking: What kind of experience have I had with this text? Have I truly engaged with it? Why have others found more in this text than I have?

Modes of Reading

It has been suggested above (and also below) that young people need to experience a whole poem several times in order to generate a meaningful response and this is an essential element of the reader response (RR) classroom. However, it is partly emphasised because recent practice has led to much outcome-based teaching where just a section of a text has been used to make an essentially linguistic point. It is not contradictory therefore to suggest that in an RR classroom, where the deeper purpose is to explore complete texts, other techniques can be used. It must also be stressed (see the guidelines above) that responding to emotionally powerful poems is difficult and demanding and students will often resist the experience, so some activities need to be 'lighter' and more 'fun', with more emphasis on the efferent aspects of a text. Treating poems as puzzles is good if this is a helpful part of a genuine RR approach.

For example:

- Giving students only the poem title and asking them to jot down their expectations
- Working on a poem for some time without giving students the title and then asking them to decide on a title; this could be done by groups as well as individuals
- Giving students just one powerful line (or two) or a striking image or example of sound and asking them to speculate on the subject or nature of the poem
- Giving students the separated verses from a longer poem or lines from a shorter poem and asking them to 'put them in order' – this can be overwhelming with some poems, so can be adapted by providing them with the 'bits' but also a copy of the whole poem with some sections complete (like a jigsaw with some of the pattern already completed)
- Giving students two poems jumbled up together and asking them to sort them out
- Giving students a poem with just a few key words 'missing'; the words themselves could be printed at the bottom of the page or displayed on the whiteboard
- Giving students a complete poem but printed in contrasting fonts and asking them to decide which font best suits the poem and why.

With all these approaches the deeper purpose can be to return to one of these poems a few lessons later and to then work with it much more 'seriously'. In this way the students already know the poem, have a 'feel' for it and have an initial response to work from, enabling a move to a fuller engagement. Returning to poems is one of the real characteristics of the RR classroom because it helps students to understand the dynamic nature of text and meaning.

Deeper Reading

Annotation and Decoration

Entering the world of the text is a process of engagement and requires the reader to draw on inner resources. Students need to take their time. Providing a copy of a poem with plenty of white space around it exemplifies the point that they can jot down words, thoughts, images, personal stories of their own, comments and questions. These 'markings' may be annotative, that is trying to reveal meaning and significance, but they might also be decorative, simply adding a pleasurable response without seeking after meaning too deeply.

Students can then return to these 'markings' at a later stage and amend and add to them – perhaps using a different colour so that they themselves can see how they are constructing a meaning over time. Equally, in the RR classroom where students are increasingly confident about interpretations being dynamic, these marked poems can be passed around so that other students can react to the reactions. In the RR classroom the responses of others are always worth considering.

Developing Reflection and Literary Reading

In order for students to become confident about response they must have time in the present tense and in retrospection. In the present tense they must have time to linger over the emergence of meaning, being able to muse, to ponder, to speculate; these are the necessary conditions for responsiveness. They must move between the world of the text, and being immersed in it, and the 'real' world where they are finding the poem's emergent significance. This is illustrated in the process above of 'marking' the text as students read and re-read. Retrospection deepens this process, for example returning to a poem and these markings a week later, and then again a week after that. On each occasion it is certain that they will have something additional to record. These single sheets are rightly fragile and ephemeral, but they represent accretions of meaning over time. A journal provides a much more lasting and substantial record of responses and responsiveness. A journal is especially pertinent to poetry because a student will read many poems over a year and, in an RR classroom, will return to these poems. A journal then becomes a developmental record of how response is generated and revised.

Sumara in his *Why Reading Literature in School Still Matters* (2002) goes a step further and asks students to write their notes on the actual book itself. This idea may fill teachers with horror at such a sacrilegious practice. But it might be argued that students making real use of a poetry anthology over a year and making it truly their own text is well worth the cost.

Enabling the Processes of Response

The types of experiential response outlined above (Engaging, Constructing, Imaging, Sounding, Embodying, Connecting and Evaluating/reflecting) are a checklist for any teacher in considering what approach to adopt with a poem to generate initial response, but they are not in any order. For example, the best initial response to a poem about a pet or animal in Year 6 may be to ask students to talk about their experiences of pets and animals. An initial response to a strongly rhymed poem with students in Year 10 might be to clap in time and sway to the poem's rhythm, in this way breaking immediately away from the analytical search for meaning and instead just 'feeling' the poem. A teacher will therefore be thinking about having a range of poems that have different characteristics and bring out certain kinds of response. Over time students become confident that they can respond and become more creative in the range of responses they can employ.

Think Aloud Protocols

Much research into children and poetry in the 1980s used a technique called 'think aloud protocol' (see especially Dias & Hayhoe, 1988). Volunteer students were provided with a cassette recorder and a poem and asked to take the equipment home and to record themselves 'thinking aloud' as they read and engaged with a poem. The insights into the way different readers articulated their thoughts provided helpful empirical evidence that the theory of reader response was sound in practice. With the development of small digital recorders, speech recognition software, laptops with a recording facility and so on, we have entered an era when children can record their responses to poetry without having to use writing or drawing. This shifts 'think aloud' from a research tool to a developmental affordance for students and teachers. Students can also store their responses and listen to them again before adding new ideas and insights into later readings. They can exchange these responses by email or put them on a secure part of the VLE. Certainly students can very easily undertake an assignment in which they create a podcast of a poem that they like, explain what appeals to them in the poem, record a reading of it and then add a few comments about its significance. Other students can download the podcast and listen to it, sending to the original student their own thoughts and perhaps a reading of the poem. To my knowledge this practice is untested and would seem very suited to KS3, but might equally well work in KS2 because the oral and aural approaches are dominant and no writing is required. In the RR classroom much emphasis is on creativity and experiment, and technology adds a powerful tool to the repertoire of the teacher and the students.

The Optimal Climate

The RR classroom puts student response first and seeks to provide a place where responding is enabled, valued and developed over time. At times it is full of energetic activity with students busily (and loudly) discussing the way to cut-up a poem or the exact word to fill a space in a single line; the pace feels fast. At other times it is absolutely silent as individuals read and re-read a particular poem or they search through an anthology for a poem that moves them; there is no 'pace', time is as absent as possible. At other, special, times a single voice is heard, investing emotion and energy in bringing a poem's significance to life for all around. On the walls are many poems and responses to poems and these both change regularly and offer an irresistible attraction for students, teachers and visitors to the classroom.

Conclusion

This is unquestionably an idealistic and profoundly aspirational picture of a classroom. It goes very much against the grain of rapid coverage of material or didactic teaching of A*-grade answers to prescribed poems. However, it is also a picture that acknowledges the reality of resistance by students themselves to deep and significant response. Such a classroom is created over time by a resilient and determined teacher and one who knows that to have all students responding is more important than any single and 'correct' answer. This teacher also knows that an experience of a poem is what matters and that means not just tolerating, but actually encouraging, diversity of response. The poem will be alive and will never be dead and buried with a definitive and final epitaph of meaning.

SOMETHING TO THINK ABOUT

'Slow reading': The emphasis in classrooms is often to get things done quickly and accurately. Should we, at least sometimes, enable children and young people to go slowly and allow them to pore over a text, to let the text sink into their minds, with no required outcome apart from them having the experience of slow and deep reading?

SOMETHING TO READ

The other chapters in this book have exciting things to say about the teaching of poetry and provide many examples of the kinds of poems that can be brought into the Reader Response classroom. A challenging read is Richard Andrews' (1991) *The Problem with Poetry* which looks very carefully at why students and teachers are often antipathetic to poetry and also looks at ways of broadening the range of poetic types we offer young people.

SOMETHING TO DO

- Try regularly (but not predictably) reading a poem aloud at the start of a lesson. Read it again at an appropriate moment during the lesson and read it once more when the main lesson is over. Leave a minute or two after the final reading for the class to let the poem sink into their minds. With some poems you may want to provide individual copies, with others you might display the poem on the whiteboard, and with some you may provide no text, thus accentuating the aural experience.

- Once you know your class well (so perhaps not in the first half term but after that) put them into 'Poetry groups', anything from three to five students. The group will then have certain tasks. For example:
  - once each half term (or every other half term if you feel this is too much) they have to select a poem of the week. This could be on any basis but many students will want more direction, such as a seasonal theme, the star sign of the month, or a current news story. The group read/perform the poem in different ways during their week and provide a large text version for the classroom wall
  - you select a strongly visual poem once a month, read it and place it on the classroom wall and one group has to provide either illustrations to accompany it or relevant pictures (occasionally this could be several or all groups at once to show the variety of responses)
  - 'word gifts': each group is responsible for an ongoing collection of words they have come across anywhere, not just in poems, and they add these words to a collection on the wall – they do not have to provide meanings. The words are a gift for anyone to use.

References

Andrews, R. (1991) *The Problem with Poetry*. Milton Keynes: The Open University Press.

Beach, R. (1993) *A Teacher's Introduction to Reader Response Theories*. Urbana, IL: NCTE.

Beach, R. & Marshall, J. (1990) *Teaching Literature in the Secondary School*. San Diego, CA: Harcourt.

Carroll, J. (2004) *Literary Darwinism: Evolution, Human Nature and Literature*. London: Taylor and Francis.

Dias, P. & Hayhoe, M. (1988) *Developing Response to Poetry*. Milton Keynes: Open University Press.

Goodwyn, A. (2010) *The Expert Teacher of English*. London: Routledge.

Goodwyn, A. Unpublished research.

Langer, J. (1995) *Envisioning Literature: Literary Understanding and Literature Instruction*. New York: Teachers' College Press.

Miall, D. (2006) *Literary Reading: Empirical and Theoretical Studies*. New York: Peter Lang.

Purves, A. & Beach, R. (1972) *Literature and the Reader: Research on Response to Literature, Reading Interests and the Teaching of Literature*. Urbana, IL: NCTE.

Richards, I.A. (1929) *Practical Criticism: A Study of Literary Judgement*. London: Routledge & Kegan Paul.

Rosenblatt, L. (1938) *Literature as Exploration*. New York: Appleton-Century.

Rosenblatt, L. (1978) *The Reader, the Text, the Poem*. Carbondale: Southern Illinois University Press.

Stevens, W. (1965) *Wallace Stevens: Selected Poems*. London: Faber and Faber.

Sumara, D. (2002) *Why Reading Literature in School Still Matters: Imagination, Interpretation, Insight*. Mahwah, NJ: Lawrence Erlbaum Associates.

Index

YOUNG CHILDREN READING

At home and at school

Rachael Levy *University of Sheffield*

Developing and supporting literacy is an absolute priority for all early years settings and primary schools, and something of a national concern. By presenting extensive research evidence, Rachael Levy shows how some of our tried and tested approaches to teaching reading may be counter-productive, and are causing some young children to lose confidence in their abilities as readers. Through challenging accepted definitions and perspectives on reading, this book encourages the reader to reflect critically on the current reading curriculum, and to consider ways in which their own practice can be developed to match the changing literacy landscape of the 21st century.

Placing the emphasis on the voices of the children themselves, the author looks at:

- what it feels like to be a reader in the digital age
- children's perceptions of reading
- home and school reading
- reading in multidimensional forms
- the future teaching of reading.

Essential reading for all trainee and practising teachers, this critical examination of a vital topic will support all those who are interested in the way we can help future generations to become literate. This book will encourage researchers and practitioners alike to redefine their own views of literacy, and situate 'reading literacy' within the digital world in which young children now live.

July 2011 • 168 pages
Cloth (978-0-85702-990-4) • £65.00
Paper (978-0-85702-991-1) • £20.99

ALSO FROM SAGE